Acknowledgements

I've had one persistent voice of encouragement in writing these pages: my beautiful bride, Jenilee. Jen, you've faithfully pushed me forward to discover and articulate the truths that have shaped our lives. The Holy Spirit's work through you has been a constant source of hope and joy to me. I could not have completed this work without your unwavering support.

Thank you, Sarah Simonic, for your encouragement and consistent editorial guidance. Your hard work and insights made writing this book a joy. Thank you, Chad Gonzales and Auxano Publications, for your commitment to excellence and aid in publishing this work.

A Reason for Hope

Stephen Samuel, Th.D.

Susan,

Thank you for the seeds you've planted.

-Stephen

A Reason For Hope
ISBN: 978-1-7354232-3-4
Copyright © 2020 Stephen Samuel, Th.D.

To my loving bride, Jenilee Samuel
And my courageous sons
Judah, Levi, Benjamin, & Shiloh

Your love and strength have fueled our journey with hope.

Table of Contents

The First Punch

"You're such an idiot!" The insult echoed from the other side of the grocery store aisle. I took a few steps around the corner to find an elementary kid looking up at his dad. His eyes were panicked with fear as his father's clenched fists and infuriated voice barked out another command. The boy had knocked over few cereal boxes and his dad was in too much of a hurry to consider the impact of his words. Dad resumed shoving his shopping cart while the little guy picked up his mess and followed. His head was bowed in discouragement as he processed through his shame.

We've all witnessed or experienced a similar scene. Our souls cringe because we all know how a moment like this can implant a life-long lie into a child's identity. A lie which will undermine confidence and cripple any future hope of wholeness.

Maybe you've heard comments like this from a parent, a spouse, or co-worker. Statements like, "You're not that important," or "Who do you think you are?" or "No one believes in you." Words like these can be dismissed as harmless, but they strike at the foundational doubts with which we all struggle.

Many of us have taken this kind of gut-punching, identity assault at a young age. As a result, we all wrestle with our worthiness before God and value before others. Are we good enough? Will God accept us? How can we earn His approval? Adding to the chains of our doubts are centuries of scriptural misunderstandings and the voices of those who aim to exploit our broken self-view.

How would you function if you believed what God knew about

you? What would your future be like if you knew the incredible identity given to you as a follower of Jesus?

As we journey into the true message of salvation, I pray you will discover freedom from the lies of unworthiness before God and firmly possess a reason for hope.

-Stephen Samuel

Author's Note:
The names of individuals and details of stories shared in this book have been altered to protect the privacy of each person.

Chapter 1
A Journey of Questions

"A prudent question is one-half of wisdom."
-Francis Bacon

"Will Jesus keep us from being killed… if we follow Him?" Her question hung in the air as she and her family waited intently for an answer. Looking at us across the small coffee table in an apartment living room, their calm demeanor was indicative of their Persian culture. We were in the Middle East, and the past three days of events had miraculously led us to dinner with this Iranian family.

Our three-day history with them began with a group prayer in our hotel lobby where we prayed for God to bring us Iranians who wanted to discover Him. After praying, we walked out of the hotel, and directly into their path. The father (let's call him Mike) scrolled through his smartphone with a concerned look while three women —his wife, daughter, and sister-in-law— were walking close behind.

My team of three approached and greeted them in Farsi saying, "Salaam Alaikum." They stopped, and the teenage daughter (let's call her Rachel) spoke with us in broken English. Using Google translate and a few comical hand gestures, we discovered they were looking for a place to stay. As we earnestly worked to communicate with them, our missionary arrived, and we invited them to have coffee with us. Mike told us they were vacationing in the area and a had place booked. Upon discovering they were from Iran, the owner canceled their reservation. As the team talked, we found another Air-BNB and booked it for them. We paid for it and gave it to them as a gift. We swapped numbers, and two days later Mike invited us to their place for dinner.

The evening meal, with all its cultural nuances, was wonderful. After our meal, we retired to the small living area to talk. Rachel looked intently at us and, as if cued by the arrival of the dessert said, "Now, tell us about Jesus." We discussed God's love for them, and through various metaphors and Scriptures communicated the meaning of a relationship with Jesus. They seemed to have difficulty understanding the idea of a personal and loving God. Then we said, "It's much like your family. God is your Father and He wants a relationship with you, just as any father wants with his children."

One of our team members shared a prophetic insight with the sister-in-law of what they felt God was saying specifically to her. Her eyes filled with tears as she realized God knew her on a personal level. At that moment, a picture of Mike at his home in Tehran flashed in my mind. I could perceive his hope to move his family to Germany. "I can see you at your house." I said to him. I described the room I saw him in and then said, "God knows your heart's desire to move your family." He looked curiously at me with no little emotional response. Afraid of offering false hope, I didn't mention the part about Germany. The family listened very intently to all we said. Then Rachel asked the hard question: "Will Jesus keep us from being killed… if we follow Him?"

I looked at our faithful missionary, hoping he would provide an answer. He looked at me and passed the challenge back to me. I was unsure of how to answer her question. If we told them Jesus would keep them from danger when they returned to Iran, they would feel betrayed when the inevitable suffering ahead would happen. If I told them the hard truth, they could refuse to accept such a life-threatening faith. The Holy Spirit nudged me to respond saying, "From the time of Jesus, his followers have suffered because of their desire to follow His teachings. No, Jesus doesn't give us a promise of safety. He only said that He would never leave us."

I pushed back tears as I remembered friends who had been killed for their faith. Everyone in the family slowly sat back in their chairs to consider the weight of our words. Our conversation continued, but we didn't feel any sense of commitment on their part. We gave them a Bible and other literature in the Farsi language. When our evening ended, the family thanked us for everything, and we expressed our hope to stay in touch with them. Walking us to the door, the mother said to us, "I had always known God (was) like this."

A few days later, I returned to the United States and had no way to communicate with our Iranian friends. Time passed and a year later, as I prepared to return to the Middle East, I got a message from our missionary. He asked if I remembered Mike's family and then joyfully reported that they had safely escaped Iran and were in Germany. The best news was that they were all following Jesus!

As I think of Rachel's question, I remember the look on her face. She posed a difficult and sincere question about placing trust in a God she could not see. You have probably thought of similar question like hers. "Can I trust God? Will He take care of me? Does He truly care?" Honest questions like this emerge at different times in our lives and are often triggered by difficult experiences. We all ask questions like these in an attempt to find a lasting hope.

I have asked the same questions and want to share how my own journey of questions and answers have shaped my relationship with Jesus and my life's work. As you read with me through my thoughts and discussions, I pray you'll discover an authentic, loving Jesus who desires to truly give you a reason for hope.

Madras (Chennai), India
1978- 1982

My story begins in the overpopulated slums of South India. Both of my parents came from Hindu backgrounds. My father often preached about the sacrifices he made in his decision to become a Christian in a Hindu culture. When he chose to follow Jesus, he cast aside his Hindu name and took on the name Samuel, as is the tradition among Indian Christians. Not long after, he went to his father in need of financial aid and was turned away. His father said, "Go to the God who gave you your name." To that God he went, and he was guided into a life of preaching the gospel.

Moving forward a few years, my parents were married, and I was the second son born into our home. By the time I arrived, my dad was a full-time evangelist traveling throughout India and Malaysia. My mom gave me the name Stephen from the scriptural account of Stephen in the book of Acts. When I was older, she soberly taught me that as the Stephen of the Scriptures laid down his life for the gospel, so I would do the same.

Church culture in India is one of saturation. We were at church almost every day, it seemed. As a little guy, I had only two concerns in life—Jesus and coffee. Not much has changed since then. My mom often recounts how I would wake up before she did and make my way down to the local street vendor's coffee outpost. Upon my arrival, the aged barista would serve up a cup of coffee-milk to me, and I would sit with the old men curiously watching their morning rituals.

My other joy in life was Jesus. Many times, late into the evening, I sat on the rooftop patio of our house and gazed up at the starry sky. I had no idea what prayer was, but I would talk with Jesus, and He would talk with me. It's possible much of it was my imagination, but I like to think God smiled at my innocence and responded in His kindness.

My earliest memory is of a dream I had. In the dream I was in a place unlike India. I was suspended in space, and before my eyes there was a rose. It was brilliant in moving colors, as if the petals were made out of a red and white light. In the dream I could only gaze upon it. It seemed to be alive. As I watched, entranced by its beauty, a drop of liquid light trickled out of its petals. Then I awoke. Immediately I ran to tell my mom my dream. She listened carefully. I asked her what she thought it was. She smiled, as if she knew more than she revealed, and said, "The rose is Jesus; He is the 'Rose of Sharon.'"[1] In my three-year-old mind it made complete sense, and I was satisfied. Today, my eyes fill with tears as I think of such a treasure God gave to me at a young age. The God I loved as a child drew near to me. Little did I know how much I would need His closeness in the years to come.

Arrival in the United States

When I was four years old, through a series of miraculous events,

1 Song of Solomon 2:1

our little family of four moved to the United States. I was too young to understand the concept of moving from one country to another. I had only heard of America a few times, and I didn't know what to expect. I remember the day we flew into John F. Kennedy Airport in New York City. As we descended, the pilot courteously said something in English, and I felt I should look out. From the center seat, I leaned toward the window to see the view. The plane descended and banked to give us a clear view of an enormous statue. There He stood in a majestic robe and Bible in one hand. In His other hand He held a flaming torch. His head was crowned with thorns. Who could it be? In my little mind I concluded this was a statue of Jesus! "Where are we?" I wondered as I watched in amazement. I later learned that the Jesus statue I had seen, of course, was the Statue of Liberty.

1986 Nederland, Texas

We were a young family in the 1980's struggling to forge a living in a camper-sized trailer. My brother and I learned English quickly but adapting to American culture took time. We didn't understand much of the culture and were naïve to the realities of a drastically different world. We were poor. We often prayed for provisions of food or toys. On more than one occasion, these provisions miraculously appeared at our door. I truly didn't know how poor we were. That reality didn't hit until the first semester of public school.

A few years after our arrival in the US, my mom was pregnant with our first sister. Her pregnancy, I later learned, went well for the first few months. Then difficulties with her blood pressure began, and doctors urged her to endure a premature delivery. She did, and our little sister entered the world two months earlier than expected. Doctors explained her enlarged bowel area was the result of an undeveloped liver. I didn't know what it meant, but we dealt with the medical issues for a full three years. Every weekend we made the two-hour drive to visit her at a government-funded hospital in Galveston, TX. Finally, she came home for a short period of time but within months, we were back to regular medical monitoring. We enjoyed her laughs, her uniquely cute smile, and her victory over so many physical battles. Time and time again, the doctors gave up hope, and God intervened because of mom and dad's prayers.

Then the sky fell. In the dark morning hours of that dreadful day, I heard my mom scream. I jolted up and out of my top bunk bed. I rushed into her room to find her wailing with grief as my dad hung up the phone. Having never seen such an emotional outburst from either parent, my brother and I waited for an explanation. Standing fearfully in our pajamas, we heard the terrible words that our sister had died a few moments earlier. My parents, brother, and younger sister kneeled around my parent's bed and did the one thing we knew to do. We prayed. We pleaded. We cried. After praying, we hurriedly grabbed our clothes and rushed out the door. In times past, we would enjoy the ocean view of the gulf and play at the back of the ferry ship as we sailed into the island. On that cold morning, however, we cried and sat silently, waiting to see the reality of what had happened. A police officer pulled us over for speeding. My dad was furious and attempted to communicate to him the reason for our urgency. He succeeded, and we arrived at the hospital, aided by a police escort. As the main lobby doors of the hospital rolled back, I remembered the story of Lazarus in the Bible. It must have been a scene similar to this one. Maybe this would be a miracle of the same nature; I tried to persuade my young self. Jesus surely could do it again.

My parents went into the room first. From my four-foot height, the room door seemed gigantic. My brother and I stepped in, and I remember watching them pull back a sheet that covered her. Peace, my three-year-old sister, lay there in a sleep-like stillness. I didn't understand what was happening. "She is only asleep," I thought to myself, "just like Jesus said about Lazarus."

I approached her bed and placed my little fingers delicately on her soft and cooled brow. She was not there. I stared at her. Her body rested before me, but she was not present. I thought I had cried all my tears on the two-hour drive, but a deeper well of sorrow erupted from my soul. We prayed to the only One who could keep this from happening. We prayed, but He did not answer.

In the days to follow, a numbing trance swallowed my heart. The following week I had to return to school. I walked up the stairway toward my class with my head bowed low. Kids were seated outside their classes, lining the hallway. As I passed by each student, their chatter silenced. A few looked up at me. I didn't like the attention. I made it to my classroom door and there stood my teacher. She looked compassionately at me, placed her hand on my shoulder, and said, "I'm so sorry Stephen." I immediately turned and bolted down the hallway into the bathroom. I cried, and cried, and cried. Crouched in the corner of the room, I began to ask the questions which follow every tragedy. What kind of a God would allow this to happen to me? Wasn't He supposed to keep evil from happening? What kind of world am I in? What kind of people would allow this to happen? What kind of God would allow this to happen?

Slowly time muted the anguish, but my wound grew deeper and mutated from grief to anger. I was broken. I feared friendships. I believed the lie that if I got too close to anyone, there was a chance that I could lose them. I resolved to never again open the door to affection. That door remained tightly shut, and my depression grew. A darkness hovered over my soul, and I didn't realize how strong it would become. From a third-grade kid to a junior in high school, I habitually shut down the emotions of my heart. A desire to be left alone consumed me. I dressed in dark colors and spoke very little. My parents, burdened with the loss of a child, the weight of poverty, and running a struggling church, tried to help me and my brother and sister as much as they could. But it wasn't enough. None of us knew how to heal.

From church tensions, to betrayals, to racism, to blatant manipulation, each year of my childhood, burdened with a sense of loss, crushed the little hope I had in God. Suicide became a common thought. I witnessed the hypocrisy of church people and the struggles we faced year after year to make a living. I watched Christian families maliciously wound our family. I watched the hostility level in our home rise. There were no safe places to hide.

My dad was a hard worker, and he rammed his work ethic into us. On the weekends, we tended to the maintenance of his small church building. I worked hard to keep my mind occupied. In my free time, I would find a dark corner in my room and simply retreat to ponder anything but the great pain in my soul. I turned to comic books. The darkness of fictional characters empathized with the darkness I felt in me.

I had no relationship with my parents. They were busy with ministry, and I felt like nothing more than an accessory to their career. My parents knew something was wrong, but they didn't know how to respond. At times my mom would quietly enter my bedroom at night. I would feign sleeping as she stood by my bed with her hands prayerfully placed on me. Convinced that venting was useless, I ignored her. My heart was cold, and it died a little more each day.

Entering my high school years, I became increasingly angry. I was not physically violent, but I felt a deep, seething rage inside. It was directed at one person—Jesus. I sat through Sunday after Sunday listening to my dad preach hundreds of the same, monotonous sermons. But the dad I saw on Sunday morning was not the dad I got at home. They were two different people. I believed I was the cause of his anger and I didn't know how or what to change. I didn't care enough to want to change.

I dreaded Saturdays, when I had to cut the lawn. I would often find our front yard littered with trash. Beer bottles, fast food remnants, dirty diapers, and other things would be scattered everywhere. I had no idea why all the garbage so frequently appeared in our yard but no one else's. Then a neighboring kid told me the reason. "It's because y'all ain't white," he said. "That's why people are throwin' trash in your yard."

His statement woke me up to the harsh reality of racism. I didn't hate white people. The few I knew didn't know much about me or my family. No one knew of the hell we had endured. This reinforced my resolve to emotionally hold people at a distance. I struggled with my grades in school. I believed the lie that I wasn't smart. That lie plagued me throughout high school.

In 1994 I turned sixteen. I knew this was supposedly a big birthday event for most Americans, but at my home, it just meant we had a cake. I still felt the weight of depression constantly pressing on my shoulders. In the summer of that year, my brother and I were introduced to a small youth group. The group's pastor was my dad's friend. They invited us to a camp called Youth for the Nations. The church group had a few cute girls in it, and that was its only appeal for me. We ventured out on a humid summer day in July toward a week that would miraculously transform my life.

We arrived at the campus of Christ for the Nations in Dallas with our youth group of fifteen kids. We were placed in a dorm room and given strict guidelines concerning camp rules. The evening rolled around, and I wearily went to the first night's event. The speaker was Gregg Johnson. After some music —which was too loud— and a skit, Gregg stepped up to the stage. I had never heard of him, but I just knew he was going to preach one of a thousand sermons that I had heard before. So I daydreamed. "Why am I here?" I thought vaguely to myself. "I don't even like these girls. They sure don't like me." Then Gregg snapped me out of my thoughts.

"Listen to me," he said. "Some of you have been fighting suicide. You have fought God, and you are angry with Him." He continued to fully describe the great wound and anger in my soul. I looked intently at him from my back-row seat and resisted his words.

"This man doesn't know what I've gone through," I thought to myself. "But God sees you," he replied as if he heard my thoughts. "Surrender to Jesus," he continued as he gave an invitation to come forward.

I sat in my chair. I had heard this speech many times before. I stood up to get a better view, and he called again, saying, "Come, Jesus wants to meet you here." Not really thinking through what I was doing, and in a seemingly involuntary response, my feet began to escort me to the front of the room. When I reached the left side of the platform, I stood gazing defiantly upward. Confusion clouded my thoughts. In desperation, I called out, "Jesus, if you really want me, I have nothing to give to you."

With that confession, I knelt down under the heavy oppressive weight on my shoulders. In a moment, I felt my heart's pain intensifying. The loss, the betrayal, the wounds all wrapped around my body like a cumulative chain of despair. Then a powerful sensation of heat, like a blanket, fell on my back. The power of that darkness broke off me. I slowly lifted my head to find that I was bowing at the feet of Jesus. There, right before me, He stood.

"Stephen," He said, "Before you were formed in your mother's womb, I called you and ordained you a prophet to the nations. Follow me." "God, I don't have anything to give to you," I replied. "Follow me," He said.

I could not see His face, but I could feel the great force of His presence penetrating every muscle in my body. I could only glimpse the intense light that pulsed from His being. At that moment, He untwisted all my darkness and fused His Spirit into me. Tears poured down my face for what seemed like hours. My body began to tremble as I bowed lower before Him. All my rage had been against Him. The Jesus before me, I realized, was much different than the one I had bitterly accused in my thoughts. When I saw Him, I knew I wanted to be with Him, and I was willing to give my life for this hope. He lovingly accepted me in my broken state.

Then the window into His realm closed, and I came back to my world. I slowly stood to find the auditorium empty. Only a few teens and leaders loitered around. Wiping away tears, I felt a sense of life in me which I had not known before. My journey of pain and fear ended, and a new journey began as I stepped out of the darkness.

September 2000: The Call to Mission

The second encounter I had with Jesus happened within a few years after I graduated high school. I was a youth pastor at a small church. I was full of zeal and lacking in direction. A fellow youth pastor invited me to bring my teens to an event in Washington DC. I knew little about it, but felt it would be a good experience for my group. The weekend event was a call to pray for the nation at the Main Mall. It was The Call DC, and I joined with over 70,000 people to fast and pray. The night before the event we made our way to a small church which opened their doors to our caravan. I, along with two other youth pastors and their groups, rallied for a night of prayer. We were all excited about attending such a historic event.

In the main sanctuary that evening, I found a quiet corner to settle down and rest. My mind flooded with concerns about my future, the ministry, broken relationships, and lacking finances. I had served as youth pastor for about two years and had grown weary of ministry. I considered resigning, finishing my college degree, and launching into a more profitable career. I knew I had a calling on my life, but the constant battles of ministry were exhausting me.

In the corner of that sanctuary, I soaked in the sounds of worship. As I whispered the familiar lyrics, "Lord, I give you my heart. I give you my soul. I live for you alone," tears trickled down my face. In frustration, I recognized my inability to go on. I thought, "God, I'm such a failure, what am I doing here?" I gazed upward at the rectangular ceiling tiles. Then from deep place of hurt within, I began to cry in earnest. I couldn't hide or deny my brokenness anymore. In the shadows of the room, I mumbled out a prayer, hoping for comfort.

In a moment, the sounds of worship became distant, and I literally left my body. I was between two worlds. Without realizing what was happening, I looked up to see the ceiling of that little church peel back to reveal another dimension. Jesus stood above me, larger and greater than I had ever imagined Him to be. With a compassionate and yet strong voice He said, "Stephen, before I formed you in your mother's womb, I called you and ordained you to be a prophet to the nations."

The intensity of His power washed over me like the waves of the ocean. I was terrified. I loved Him, but the One before me was much greater and more astonishing than I had ever thought He was. When He said, "I ordained you to be a prophet to the nations," I saw the entire world for a moment. A small, white streak of light moved from one location on the globe to another. I understood it was my mandate to go to preach the Gospel in many nations.

I looked down, and for a moment wanted to crawl under the frail church pew behind me, but I could not move. I could feel Him around me and within me. It was like my imagination and every thought, every facet of me, was fully aware of Him. I struggled to keep my gaze upon Him. His face poured out an intense, piercing white light. His eyes were brilliantly blue with a burning orange fire in them. I couldn't see His form; His presence was nearly impossible to fully capture with my limited senses.

With all the strength I had, I pushed my head upward to see Him again. As I did, the entire scene vanished just as quickly as it began.

I sat there staring again at a white ceiling. I laid on my face feeling like I had been in His presence for hours. It probably was only a few minutes. My whole body shook as I wobbled upward and made my way toward my group.

Since that day, my purpose has been clear. I have found myself traveling to the most remote of regions telling the story of how Jesus found me. As I look back on my early years of ministry, I remember so many stories and revelations that firmly laid my foundation of faith. This relationship I have with Jesus began in a time of my greatest despair. In my brokenness He spoke to me, and my life has been transformed.

I close this chapter with the words of the Apostle Peter's directive to the Church. He writes, "…be ready always to give an answer to every man that asks you a reason of the hope that is in you." (1 Peter 3:15) Peter encourages us to be prepared with a defense for the faith we have. We are encouraged to provide this to everyone who asks for a "reason of the hope" in us. The word *reason* is defined as a "narrative account; a record or description of past events."[2] In essence, he is saying we should be able to give a defense for our faith to everyone who asks for the story of how we came to believe the truths we hold. We all have a story which has led us to a composition of our beliefs and resulting lifestyle. Though it is foolish to accept truth solely on our experience, experiences must cohere with the truths we claim to believe.

I've shared some of my story and hope to unveil more as I lay the foundation for the faith, which has guided me. In the chapters ahead, I will utilize the framework of the Apostle Paul's Galatian letter to unfold relevant truths concerning salvation. Paul's message concern-

2 Thompson, J. (2015). Bible Sense Lexicon: Dataset Documentation. Bellingham, WA: Faithlife.

ing God's righteous nature in the believer is often misunderstood. Because of this many have felt deficient in the hope they need to fulfill their life's purpose. My desire is to unfold the gospel to you in a way which will empower you to experience an intimate relationship with Jesus. To begin, let's start with the historical backdrop upon which Paul wrote his first letter.

Chapter 2
The First Letter

"To be convinced in our hearts that we have forgiveness of sins
and peace with God by grace alone is the hardest thing. By faith we
began, by hope we continue, and by revelation we shall obtain the
whole."
-Martin Luther

Paul's letter to the Galatians formed a simple and enduring foundation to understanding our relationship with God. The importance of this letter is evidenced by the place it takes as the first of the New Testament letters written to a newly forming church. Before the gospel of Mark, which is believed to be the earliest of the gospels, Galatians was penned to a mostly non-Jewish population. Historians date the authorship of Galatians to be as early as 44 AD or as late as 49 AD. This early date also emphasizes how the Christian movement rapidly exploded across the known world before any biographical text concerning Jesus emerged.

Some suggest the letter of James (or Jakob), the brother of Jesus, may have preceded Galatians, but Paul's first letter was dispersed within this same time. There are also some minor speculations in the gospel community that Paul wrote to the Thessalonians before Galatians, but the majority of evidence indicates this scenario is unlikely with regard to the chronology of Paul's travel which is provided to us by Luke. To understand the history before Paul's letter, below is a brief timeline of events prior to his authorship of Galatians.

Autumn 47–Spring 48 AD	Paul in Antioch of Syria in (Acts 12:25–13:1)
April 48–September 49	First missionary journey (Acts 13–14)
April 48	Departure from Antioch of Syria
April–June 48	Visit to Cyprus
July 48	Visit to Pamphylia
July–September 48	Visit to Pisidian Antioch
October 48- February 49	Visit to Iconium
March - June 49	Visit to Lystra & Derbe
June–August 49	Return visit to churches
Autumn 49	Return to Antioch of Syria
Autumn 49	Peter at Antioch (Gal 2:11–16)
Autumn 49	Galatians written from Antioch
Autumn 49	Jerusalem council, Paul's third visit (Acts 15)[3]

In the appendix, I inserted a brief overview of the three common theories which detail the dating of the Galatian letter. Moving forward, it will benefit us to know Paul's backstory.

---

3 Hoehner, H. W. (1996). Chronology of the New Testament. In D. R. W. Wood, I. H. Marshall, A. R. Millard, J. I. Packer, & D. J. Wiseman (Eds.), New Bible dictionary (3rd ed., p. 198). Leicester, England; Downers Grove, IL: InterVarsity Press.

Paul's History With The Church

To introduce himself in Galatians, Paul guided his readers through his brief history (Galatians 1:13-16). He began with his conversion experience, (Acts 9:1-9) then told of his departure from Jerusalem to Damascus. (Galatians 1:17, Acts 9:20-25) From there he journeyed to Arabia and remained there for three years before returning to Damascus. Shortly after his arrival there, he was opposed for his message of salvation through Jesus. He escaped persecution and journeyed south to Jerusalem to see the apostle Peter. After visiting with him, Paul mentioned his visit with James, the brother of Jesus.

At this point, many in the church were still not convinced of Paul's conversion. From Jerusalem he voyaged back to his hometown of Tarsus and remained there for nine years. Then Barnabas, a well-trusted apostle in Jerusalem, journeyed north with the sole intent of finding Paul. Barnabas found him in Tarsus and then took him to Antioch in Syria where they cultivated the church for a full year (Acts 11:26).

During this time, a great famine afflicted Jerusalem; the church of Antioch responded by sending financial aid and chose Paul and Barnabas to take the funds to Jerusalem. After delivering the aid, Paul, Barnabas and newcomer John Mark returned to Antioch. They were then commissioned to take the gospel to the Gentiles in the Galatian region. They proceeded west to the Island of Cypress to begin their first missionary journey. From Cypress they traveled north to the regions of Paphos, Perga, Pamphylia and then to Antioch of Pisidia. After this, their journey turned southward as they visited the cities of Iconium, Lystra, Derbe, and finally, they returned to Antioch in Syria.

After fourteen years of travel Paul returned to Jerusalem with his companions Titus and Barnabas. They were met with some resistance by those in the church who felt Titus, a Greek, had to obey the tradition of circumcision to be a follower of Jesus. Paul vehemently objected and took it up with the apostles Peter and James. This conflict could have been the first of many situations which fueled Paul to make clear the gospel message. Following Paul's passionate defense of Titus, James recognized the call of God on Paul. The Jerusalem church then commissioned him to go out with a directive to encourage the Gentile Church and to take care of the poor.

Hearing about the expansion of the Church in Antioch, Peter visited Paul. When Peter arrived, Paul confronted him on the issue of Peter's refusal to eat with Gentiles in the presence of devout Jews. Peter's hypocritical standard invoked a response that clarified how righteousness is acquired under the new covenant. Paul rebuked Peter in the company of all the church saying, "A man is not justified by the works of the law but by faith in Jesus Christ." He summarized the fundamental nature of the gospel by stating how we are "justified by faith in Christ and not by the works of the law; for by the works of the law no flesh will be justified." (Galatians 2:16)

Paul's statement was a direct contradiction to centuries of Judaism's teachings. Under the Old Testament, righteousness (or right standing) with God was a result of one's ability to keep the moral law. From the eating of approved animals to ceremoniously approaching God in sacred manner, every Jew bowed to the behavioral prescriptions of the law. Paul had thoroughly studied and taught the laws of Moses. He was an expert in the right and wrong ways to think and behave. But now, with his new revelation, Paul explained a far simpler pathway to becoming justified before God. He writes how he lived by "faith in the Son of God" (Galatians 2:20).

By rejecting his life-long devotion to Judaism, Paul offered a hope of possessing salvation outside of the demands of the moral law. In the face of great controversy, Paul taught that one could not attain right standing with God simply by good behavior. He cautioned his readers to not disregard the moral law because of Christ's work, rather, because of Jesus' resurrection, believers were empowered to keep God's law. In short, Paul introduced righteousness not as a keeping or breaking of the law, but as a result of faith in Jesus.

This simple message, which we'll unfold in the following chapters, was the revelation Paul was commissioned to preach. He felt appointed to make this truth well-known throughout the newly forming Christian church each time he took up his pen to write. With this in mind, we can see the reason for Paul's passion in this letter. He begins with his well-known introduction, "Paul an Apostle..." (Galatians 1:1).

The Apostle

The title *Apostle* marks the nature of Paul's role in the first century. Apostle, meaning "one who is sent," was taken from the prevailing Hellenistic-Greek culture in Galatia years before the birth of Christ. The title became common during the conquest of Alexander the Great (336 BC). As his empire stretched across the ancient world, young Alexander made periodic visits to his conquered regions. As expected, the subjugated communities resisted his hopes of assimilation. To overcome this, Alexander would send out an emissary team ahead of his arrival. This team of "apostles" would arrive months, or even years, before Alexander. They effectively taught the Greek-Hellenistic culture, language, and traditions to the people, with the aim

31

of undermining the indigenous culture. This known practice of hostile assimilation was previously thrust on the Jews by the Assyrians around 726 BC (2 Kings 17:6). Although the Assyrians failed in their attempt to marginalize the Jewish culture, it seems the Greeks were far more effective.

With this historical context of an apostle, Jesus coined the title to define the role of His own disciples. They were to go before Him to prepare communities for His visit. The apostles of Jesus were given an eternal mandate to replace cultural traditions and beliefs with the ethics of the Kingdom of Heaven (Luke 10:1-11). With this same conviction and calling, Paul established his authority as an apostle "not from men nor through man, but through Jesus Christ and God the Father who raised Him from the dead" (Galatians 1:1).

Throughout history Paul's letter, though composed over a few brief pages, has profoundly impacted key leaders in the faith. Martin Luther (1483-1546) said, "The little book of Galatians is my letter; I have betrothed myself to it; it is my wife."[4] Centuries later, John Wesley (1703-1791) declared how he found "Personal lasting peace from a sermon on Galatians."[5] These men re-discovered the simplicity of the gospel message as Paul had intended it to be understood.

Their discoveries led them to unveil the gospel in an effective way to their respective generations. The revelations they preached directly conflicted with the traditional religious teachings of their day. They followed the example Paul set in his writing of Galatians. He contradicted centuries of traditional views concerning righteousness before God.

But who were the recipients of this first letter? To answer this, we

4 Utley, R. J. (1997). Paul's First Letters: Galatians and I & II Thessalonians (Vol. Volume 11, p. 1). Marshall, TX: Bible Lessons International.
5 Ibid

can turn to the brief accounts of cities which Paul visited on his first missionary journey through the Galatia region.

Who Were the Galatians?

Paul began his first missionary journey during the height of Roman political power. Through numerous resources made available to church communities today, we know about the Biblical culture of Israel. However, much remains uncirculated about the Greek and Roman communities which shaped Israel and the nations around it. The land of Galatia derived its name from the people of Gaul who were forcibly migrated there from the ancient region of Thrace (Bulgaria). Under the influence of Greeks, they were identified as Thracians. Following the Greek occupation, the Thracians were conquered by the Romans around AD 42. They gradually lost their self-governing powers as Roman authority intensified throughout the world. Not long after the Roman armies had trampled through Galatia, the apostles of Jesus arrived to plant the seeds of the New Testament Church.

When the message of a Jewish, death-defying Son of God came to them, it was amidst the oppression of an occupying military force. Because of this, the hope of a Greek or Roman god appearing among them to bring deliverance, was not a far-fetched hope. The weariness of oppression may have paved the way for a saving deity to be received, but there was a disturbing downside to the Galatians superstitious culture. It seems their fears were easily swayed by the voices of religious leaders who sought to manipulate them. One can see how the Galatians readily accepted the gospel and at times violently rejected the apostles within days of their welcome.

To compound their fears, the cities of Galatia were frequently trafficked by a variety of cultural and religious movements. Located along the Great Silk Road, a continent-spanning trade route, Galatia served to be a regular stop for peddlers of new philosophies and faiths. These communities were the breeding grounds of mystic conquerors as well as political ones. Trade routes were not merely a place to exchange merchandise, but they served as a pathway by which knowledge traveled from one part of the world to another.

In spite of these influences, one hears the hope of Paul's introductory comment as he introduces Jesus to be the one who came to deliver the Galatians "from this present evil world" (Galatians 1:4). They sought a deliverer to redeem them from the onslaught of religious Jews, Greek mystics, and Roman power.

As the gospel message displaced numerous philosophies and beliefs, the people of Gaul nurtured this new faith in Jesus until it became one which overthrew the greater political and religious ideologies of the day. Before we look at the letter of Galatians, it may serve us to peer into the history of the Galatian cities.

Paul's first missionary journey through Galatia originated in the city of Antioch, near the Syrian border. He and Barnabas were commissioned by the Holy Spirit to go west to the Island of Cyprus and then north to the region of Pamphylia. As they departed Paphos, their young assistant, John Mark, departed from them and returned to Jerusalem while Paul and Barnabas continued north until they reached their next city, called Antioch of Pisidia.

Antioch of Pisidia

In Antioch of Pisidia Paul was invited by the leaders of the synagogue to share "any word of exhortation for the people" (Acts 13:15).

Like any good preacher, Paul couldn't pass up the opportunity. He took the stage and taught an abbreviated summary of the Old Testament. Paul began with the deliverance of Israel from Egypt to its Judges, and then to the promise God made to King David of a Savior to come. He concluded by describing how Jesus was taken and killed by the Jews and then rose from the dead. His resurrection was not only for Israel, but for anyone who would believe in Him. Paul explained how each believer could be justified, or made right, with God. The Jews, he pointed out, could not be justified by Moses' law, but now, by believing in Jesus, this new place of right standing with God could be attained.

This was one of the first times the gospel was clearly laid out to the Jews in Antioch. The response was affirming! They asked Paul and Barnabas to return the following week to preach again, and the entire city showed up to hear Paul. As a result of the mass response, the Jewish leaders grew envious of Paul and began to contradict and resist his teaching. In response to the mounting tension from the unbelieving Jews, Paul responded by saying, "It was necessary that the word of God should be spoken to you first; but since you reject it, and judge yourselves unworthy of everlasting life, behold, we turn to the Gentiles" (Acts 13:46).

It seems the Jews were content to hear any encouraging words from Paul and Barnabas, but when the popularity of their message threatened their religious authority, it seemed they wanted nothing to do with the apostles. In response to the rejection by the Jewish leaders, Paul and Barnabas moved from the Pisidia region and traveled south to Iconium.

Iconium

Iconium, known today as Konya, was a principle city in the southern part of the Roman region of Galatia. This city struggled with its identity for many years. It belonged to the "Phrygian region" as mentioned in Acts 16:6. The emperor Claudius (10 BC – AD 54) conferred on it the title Claudiconium, which appeared on coins of the city and on inscriptions, and was formerly taken as a proof that Claudius raised the city to the rank of a Roman Colonia. Then Emperor Hadrian (76 AD -138 AD) gave the city a more prominent title, evidenced by its new name, Colonia Aelia Hadriana Iconiensium. These facts tell us Iconium was a Hellenistic city, but it held a strong pro-Roman bias when Paul visited it. [6]

As we know, Barnabas and Paul's arrival in the city was due to the persecution they faced in Antioch of Pisidia. Entering the city, they followed their normal practice of visiting the synagogue. In response, "a great multitude both of the Jews and of the Greeks believed" (Acts 14:1). Their ministry, however, was not without trouble as unbelieving Jews stirred the Iconians against Paul. Unlike their response in the previous town, Paul "stayed there a long time, speaking boldly in the Lord, who was bearing witness to the word of His grace, granting signs and wonders to be done by their hands" (Acts 14:3). The aggression against Paul and Barnabas continued to increase until a "violent attempt was made by both the Gentiles and Jews, with their rulers, to abuse and stone them." When Paul received news of this, they escaped to the city of Lystra.

Lystra

Entering Lystra, Paul came upon a crippled man and perceived the man had faith to be healed. Paul declared, "Stand up straight on your feet!" The crippled man jumped up, and the entire communi-

6 https://www.bible-history.com/isbe/i/iconium/
7 Acts 14:10 (NKJV).

ty reeled in astonishment. The display of Paul's supernatural power provoked an explosive response. "The gods have come down to us in the likeness of men," the Lycaonians declared.[8] It seemed their underlying mythological hopes were affirmed. In a rush of enthusiasm, they declared Barnabas to be Zeus and Paul to be Hermes. The priests of the temple brought oxen and garlands, and the apostles "could scarcely restrain them from sacrificing to them." [9]

In a few short days, however, the winds of popularity turned against them. The Jews from Antioch and Iconium entered Lystra to persuade the multitude against the apostles. The mob responded by stoning Paul and dragging his body outside of the city. They left him for dead. The Lycaonians' dramatic shift from worshipping the apostles as gods to condemning them to death shed light on how easily they were ruled by popular opinion. Although we do not fully know what message the Jewish leaders propagated to sway the Lycaonians, we can conclude the people were extremely volatile in their loyalty.

After the tumult ended, a few disciples gathered around Paul's body and watched him miraculously stand up and walk back into the city. The following day, Paul and Barnabas moved forward to the city of Derbe. However, it is important to note that in view of all this activity, Paul also met with young Timothy, a third-generation follower of Jesus, in this city.

Derbe & Antioch of Syria

Derbe served to be a staging point from which the apostles traveled back and forth to Iconium and Antioch of Pisidia. Although not much is said about Derbe, we find the apostles had a healthy time of respite there. From this city they traveled to nearby areas to "strengthen the souls of the disciples (Acts 14:22). From Derbe, Paul

8 Acts 14:11. (NKJV).
9 Acts 14:18 (NKJV).

made his way through Pisidia and then on to Pamphlia, Perga, and Attalia. His journey concluded in the city of Antioch in Syria. He "stayed there a long time with the disciples" (Acts 14:28).

Antioch, as we later discover, would serve as the hub from which many of the New Testament epistles would be copied and distributed. The city of Antioch was founded in 300 BC and then conquered by Pompey in 64 BC. It was made capital of the Roman province of Syria. In the first century it was the third largest city of the Roman Empire, with a population comprised of Syrians, Greeks, Jews and Romans. Following the death of Stephen (34 AD), the first Christian martyr, the gospel was first preached in Antioch to Gentiles as well as Jews with great success (Act 11:19–21). From Antioch Barnabas and Paul were sent out to engage in wider evangelistic activity. Antioch remained the base for Paul's work for many years.

Though more could be written about these cities, these simple snapshots give us insight into the people who first received the gospel of Jesus. What opened their hearts to receive the teachings of salvation? To answer this, we must turn to the actual message they heard. We can unfold Paul's message from the questions he asked them.

Chapter 3
Salvation: The Union of God and Man

"Embodiment is the end of God's path."
- Friedrich Christoph Oetinger

Following a few brief sentences of introduction (Galatians 1:1-5), Paul reasoned his way through the broken beliefs which had led his readers to accept heretical teachings. His direct approach may have sounded blunt, but considering the labor he poured into the Galatian community, we can empathize with his frustration. In his line of questioning, Paul laid for us the foundation of well-understood truths concerning salvation. We can presume he taught these truths to the early church as we read of his zealous reaction.

"How did you receive the Spirit?" he asked. His question exposed a bedrock truth about salvation. When a follower of Jesus begins with their commitment, a spiritual union occurs. Every believer receives the voice of the Holy Spirit into his or her consciousness. Why should you note this? Because, the idea of a human spirit and the Spirit of God becoming unified in one body was a far stretch for the ancient world.

During the time of Paul's writing, false beliefs arose to challenge the reality of God indwelling the human body. This idea, though not completely foreign, has been minimized in the historical progression of the Christian faith. Within 350 years of Paul's writing, the church

Father Augustine of Hippo expressed amazement at the possibility of God living in men and women. In his Confessions he wrote, "And what room is there within me, whither my God can come into me? Whither can God come into me, God who made heaven and earth? Is there, indeed, O Lord my God, aught in me that can contain Thee?"[10]

The greatness of God merging Himself into in the temporal human body should invoke humility on our part. However, many advocate a false humility by discarding this belief and assuming God's indwelling is merely metaphorical. It is easier to believe God's mind is preoccupied with matters of greater spiritual significance than our mediocre cares. But He is concerned and fully engaged in our every passing moment. Jesus reveals God's detailed concern for us by saying He accounts for every hair on our head (Luke 12:7). He shows us that God's interest involves even the trivial concerns of what we eat and wear. God became a man, not to show us His disdain for humanity, but to show His extreme value for us (Romans 5:8).

God's desire has always been to coexist with us. From the Garden of Eden to His visit at Mount Sinai (Exodus 24), to the incarnation of Jesus, He has broadcast His desire to live among us. The message of the gospel is how God made His desire a reality. God came near to us by placing Himself in us. This was the point of Paul's first question. How were the Galatians infused with God's Spirit? Was it by keeping the moral Law, or by believing Jesus made a way for His Spirit to live in them?

Paul's question establishes the true nature of salvation for us. God came to live as a man so man could live with God in him. This promise of God's Spirit living in us is expressed initially in Isaiah's

10 Augustine, S., Bishop of Hippo. (1996). The Confessions of St. Augustine. (E. B. Pusey, Trans.). Oak Harbor, WA: Logos Research Systems, Inc.

prophetic description of Jesus. Isaiah called Him Emmanuel, which means "God with us."[11] Though Isaiah's prediction speaks about Jesus specifically, we can see the continuation of God's coexistence in the believer. Paul reveals how, "Christ in you" is the "the hope of glory." (Colossians 1:27). This thought is repeated again and again in the New Testament letters. (See Romans 8:10, Ephesians 3:16, Colossians 3:16). This joining of God's Spirit with our own spirit is a miraculous event. However, this miracle is often reduced to a momentary act of confession. To fully understand the profound value of salvation, let's dive into the relational transaction one experiences at the point of salvation.

How Did You Get "Saved"?

If you've been exposed to protestant church culture for any extended period of time, you may have found yourself experiencing what many refer to as an "altar call." It's the portion of a meeting, usually during the conclusion, in which a speaker invites his or her audience to respond to the message of salvation. This practice dates back to the revivalist Charles G. Finney (1792 – 1875). Altar calls, though significantly different in Finney's day, have evolved into a moment when one can "be saved" if he or she responds in repentance. Respondents are usually led in prayer to ask for the forgiveness of their sins and make a commitment to follow Jesus.

This form of "receiving" salvation, however, is not found in the Scriptures or in any record of the early Church. Of the few accounts we have recorded of recipients deciding to believe in the teachings of the apostles, they were directly asked to believe in Jesus and profess their belief. Following this, the Holy Spirit would often move upon believers to validate their salvation experience. In response to God's Spirit, many are recorded to have obeyed in the prophetic act of bap-

11 Strong, J. (1995). Enhanced Strong's Lexicon. Woodside Bible Fellowship.

tism (Acts 8:12-13, 8:37, Acts 11:15-18, Acts 11:21, Acts 13:48-52, Acts 16:30-34). According to the New Testament record, we repeatedly see those who wanted to follow Jesus respond in faith by professing their belief in Him. Nothing more was required.

Paul clarified the transaction of salvation in his letter to the Ephesians when he wrote, "For by grace you have been saved through faith, and that not of yourselves; it is the gift of God..." (Ephesians 2:8). He revealed a two-part relational exchange which occured at the point of salvation. First, God enables us to perceive our need for Him. The Holy Spirit directly influences us with the ability to recognize His love and desire to redeem us from our sinful nature.

We see this in the phrase Paul used to indicate the means by which we are saved. He says it is "by grace." The word grace is defined as a "Divine influence upon the heart, and its reflection in the life."[12] This means God draws us to salvation by His Spirit. He draws all who will allow themselves to be influenced by His love.

The second part of this relational interaction is faith. Faith is one's response to God's drawing grace. When we believe God is inviting us into a relationship, then faith is awakened in us and the seed of salvation is made alive. Everyone has some "measure of faith" to believe.[13] Like a lifeguard reaching out to a drowning victim, God extends His hand of grace to us. In response, we extend our faith to Him to be saved.

Knowing this, we can ask a subsequent question. What can we expect as an evidence of one's salvation? Consider these twelve records of salvation responses in the New Testament Church.

---

12 Strong, J. (2009). A Concise Dictionary of the Words in the Greek Testament and The Hebrew Bible (Vol. 1, p. 77). Bellingham, WA: Logos Bible Software.
13 The New King James Version. (1982). (Ro 12:3). Nashville: Thomas Nelson.

Acts 2:41

Then those who gladly received his word were baptized; and
that day about three thousand souls were added to them.

Acts 4:4

However, many of those who heard the word believed; and
the number of the men came to be about five thousand.

Acts 4:32

Now the multitude of those who believed were of one heart
and one soul; neither did anyone say that any of the things he
possessed was his own, but they had all things in common.

Acts 5:14–15

And believers were increasingly added to the Lord, multi-
tudes of both men and women, so that they brought the sick
out into the streets and laid them on beds and couches, that
at least the shadow of Peter passing by might fall on some of
them.

Acts 8:12-13

But when they believed Philip as he preached the things concerning the kingdom of God and the name of Jesus Christ,
both men and women were baptized. Then Simon himself
also believed; and when he was baptized, he continued with
Philip, and was amazed, seeing the miracles and signs, which
were done.

Acts 8:37

Then Philip said, "If you believe with all your heart, you may."
And he answered and said, "I believe that Jesus Christ is the

Son of God." So, he commanded the chariot to stand still. And both Philip and the eunuch went down into the water, and he baptized him.

Acts 9:17

And Ananias went his way and entered the house; and laying his hands on him he said, "Brother Saul, the Lord Jesus, who appeared to you on the road as you came, has sent me that you may receive your sight and be filled with the Holy Spirit."

Acts 10:44–47

While Peter was still speaking these words, the Holy Spirit fell upon all those who heard the word. And those of the circumcision who believed were astonished, as many as came with Peter, because the gift of the Holy Spirit had been poured out on the Gentiles also. For they heard them speak with tongues and magnify God. Then Peter answered, "Can anyone forbid water, that these should not be baptized who have received the Holy Spirit just as we have?"

Acts 16:31–33

So they said, "Believe on the Lord Jesus Christ, and you will be saved, you and your household." Then they spoke the word of the Lord to him and to all who were in his house. And he took them the same hour of the night and washed their stripes. And immediately he and all his family were baptized.

Acts 19:1–2

And it happened, while Apollos was at Corinth, that Paul, having passed through the upper regions, came to Ephesus. And finding some disciples he said to them, "Did you receive the Holy Spirit when you believed?"

Acts 19:18
And many who had believed came confessing and telling
their deeds.

From these records we can see three common truths about salvation. First, everyone believed what they heard about Jesus. We don't
see a prolonged confession of past sins. We don't read of commit-
ments made to live a moral life. We don't read of the fear of eternal
damnation motivating hearers to receive Jesus. I make this point because often confessions of faith are cloaked in a fear of judgement or
a resolution to be a better person. Many believers begin their walk
with Jesus out of fear. As a result, believers often live under a nagging
need to repeatedly repent of their sins.

*If maintaining righteousness or moral behavior is the focus of a
Christian's life, then there must always be an awareness of the behaviors to avoid.* When we are plagued by how we may disappoint God
with our behavior, it produces in our soul an underlying sense of
failure. Paul defines this thought process as condemnation (Romans
8:1).

Although the moral law, which God has placed in the soul of
every man, drives us to be a better person, awareness of our broken,
sinful nature isn't enough. A resolution to be a better person will not
produce the righteous nature of God in us. The moral law doesn't
provide the power to overcome one's propensity to sin.

Paul's message and the history of the early church speak to this
moral dilemma: We no longer need to live trapped under the con-

demnation of sin and our inability to be good (Galatians 5:1-6). Rather, we can believe in Jesus' atonement for us and be freed from sin and its consequences. When you believe God's identity has been deposited into your life, then you, by faith, meet all the requirements needed to sustain relationship with Him.

In our salvation, Jesus places His righteous identity into the consciousness of everyone who will believe in Him. He is perfect and He fulfilled all God's requirements for humanity to have a relationship with God. We only have to believe that God loved us, and because of His love, He made sin powerless in its ability to separate us from Himself.

Let me clarify a brief point on this matter. The message of salvation has often been minimized to the confession of sins. This reduced theology leads believers to linger in an awareness of past sinful behavior. When we are conscious of our sin, the process of self-evaluation can become dominating and lead our thoughts to be perpetually self-condemning. As a result, we will not find ourselves believing we have God's nature within us. We'll always feel like we are reaching for a righteousness we don't have. This trap of repeated confession to sustain righteousness is the struggle that drives many to live under a weight of guilt and shame.

The struggle to confess sin and be sinless before God tormented the reformer Martin Luther. His overly sensitive conscience drove him to a place of despondency. It is known that "Luther would drive himself and his confessor half-mad with his endless confessions, which seemed to make him feel no better, because he would torture himself afterward, feeling that surely he must have forgotten something."[14] In the torment of guilt, he discovered a life-changing revela-

14 Metaxes, Eric. Martin Luther. (New York: Viking 2017)

tion. He realized he could only be justified by faith in Jesus. Luther's great discovery lay in realizing that he was made right with God by faith and not by his devoted behavior.

In the book *Luther,* by Eric Metaxes, I was amused to discover when Luther's epiphany came. He found his revelation while he was on the toilet. I laughed for a full day after reading this. The wisdom and great righteousness God unveiled to Luther was in the humiliation of a bathroom. God unfolded His victory over sin's power and overturned the entire religious system of the Medieval era by unlocking a simple revelation to a monk on a toilet. God impressed upon Luther how he could receive righteousness if he only would believe it was given to him. Luther's liberation came through the understanding of six words. "The just shall live by faith."[15] This same righteousness or identity of God is placed in every believer as a result of faith in Jesus. As Luther was delivered from the bondage of feeling unrighteous before God, so everyone can find the freedom Jesus offers to all who will believe.

What then should happen after one is forgiven of his or her sins? Does the Christian life merely become a moral dance between sin and repentance? The awareness of sins to avoid tends to only perpetuate a cycle of failing, then condemnation and then confession. This cycle becomes the pattern of behavior for many believers when they don't realize what happened in the death and resurrection of Jesus.

When you hear of believers perpetually fighting sin, they are betraying a partial understanding of God's identity in themselves. When a disciple does not know they possess the righteous nature of God, it prevents them from living in the fulfillment they were created to enjoy. You have been freed to enjoy unobstructed communica-

15 The New King James Version. (1982). (Ro 1:17). Nashville: Thomas Nelson.

tion and approval from God. God's righteous nature has been placed in you. This is the work of salvation.

What should a saved life look like? It should look like Jesus' life. Jesus experienced the full approval of God and demonstrated to us how we can have the same. As Dallas Willard points out in his book Spirit of the Disciplines, Jesus lived in the Kingdom of Heaven. This Kingdom is the realm of constant coexistence with the Father. This was the point of Jesus' incarnation. Willard says,

> Christ's transcendent life in the present Kingdom of Heaven is what drew the disciples together around Jesus prior to his death. And then resurrection and post-resurrection events proved that life to be indestructible. They verified that all of Jesus' teachings about life in the Kingdom were true. The cross, which was always present in their thought and experience, came to the center because the force of the higher life was allowed to dissipate as the generations passed by. Eyewitnesses—the people who had seen and felt the transcendent life—were no longer there to convey it and tell of it firsthand. That "hands on" viewpoint was replaced with another. The church's understanding of salvation then slowly narrowed down to a mere forgiveness of sins, leading to heaven beyond this life. And Christ's death came to be regarded as only the merit-supplying means to that forgiveness, not as the point where his life was most fully displayed and triumphant, forever breaking the power of sin over concrete human existence. [16]

Secondly, we see from the list of passages in Acts that believers were physically baptized. To the Jews, baptism was not a foreign

---

16 Willard, Dallas. The Spirit of the Disciplines. (San Francisco: Harper One, 1999), 35-36.

practice. The temple of Jesus' day had designated locations for baptisms in accordance with the tradition of the Mikveh. *Mikveh* is the term for a pool of water used for baptism. Jewish custom called for devout followers of Yahweh to be spiritually cleansed in preparation for events such as weddings, performing temple duties, or on the eve of Yom Kippur. Baptism served as a sign of commitment to the God of Israel. With this practical background, Jewish apostles, following Jesus' command, affirmed the need for new believers to be baptized.

The underwater immersion made evident the ending of an old state of being and the beginning of a new one. It was a visible declaration of devotion. As the New Testament church utilized this practice, it served to be a prophetic act which defined laying down one's old identity and being born into the identity of Jesus. I describe baptism as a prophetic act rather than a symbolic ceremony because it physically demonstrates one dying to their identity and rising again in Christ's identity. In believing that one's action in baptism reflects their actions of faith, the power of baptism exceeds a mere symbol. It is much more than a traditional induction into a church club. It is a lifelong commitment to live in the new nature.

Thirdly, believers experienced a physical interaction as God's Spirit entered into them. Moments of conversion were marked by prophetic utterances or by speech in an unfamiliar language. This supernatural phenomenon experienced by believers is often equated to "being filled with the Holy Spirit." We find this miracle occurring repeatedly in the book of Acts (Acts 1:8, 4:8, 4:31, 6:3, 6:5, 7:55, 8:17, 9:17, 10:44-47, 11:15, 19:5-6).

What does it mean to be *filled with the Holy Spirit?* As we discussed previously, it is the essence of salvation. God extends to us

His grace, and we respond in faith. In this faith, He places in us His Spirit. Paul, in his following letter to the Corinthians, describes this powerful union of God's Spirit with our spirit as having a similar potency to the sexual and emotional union between a man and a woman (1 Cor. 6:17). He implies that as a man and woman are united in one body, we are united in Spirit with the Lord.

This miraculous union was not available to humanity before Christ's atonement. This makes our realization of Jesus' death and resurrection even more important. Jesus died to make room for His Divine Self to inhabit our human consciousness. In His concluding discussion with His disciples in John 14, Jesus clearly defines how salvation would be made accessible to them. He said to them,

Let not your heart be troubled. You believe in God, believe also in Me. In my Father's house are many mansions and I go there to prepare a place for you. And if I go and prepare a place for you, I will come again and receive you to Myself; that where I am, there you may be also. And where I go you know, and the way you know. – John 14:1-4

This text paints a clear picture of salvation. I remember the first time I stumbled upon the deeper meaning of this. I was a young preacher conducting a funeral for a family in our church. Standing on the cemetery lawn, I opened my small Bible to the familiar passage of John 14. As I read it aloud, the passage didn't settle well with my soul. What was I offering this family amidst their whirlwind of grief and pain? Was I proposing heavenly real estate as a consolation?

Driving home from the funeral service, insight from Holy Spirit came to me. He explained to me, "Jesus offered to His disciples an explanation for His suffering, not the hope of an eternal retirement." Jesus was telling His disciples about the ability they would soon have, to commune with the Father at any time as a result of His death and resurrection. The "mansion" He offered is not a house in heaven. The word mansion is better translated as a "dwelling place" or "place of rest" within one's consciousness. We can understand that this passage does not speak of a heavenly retirement home because Jesus said it will be the place where He comes to us (John 14:23).

This place is accessible to us at any time in any place. Jesus continued with saying, "A little while longer and the world will see Me no more, but you will see Me. Because I live, you will live also. At that day you will know that I am in My Father, and you in Me, and I in you" (John 14:19-20). What did He mean by this? Again, He was telling us of the accessibility a believer will have to be able to consciously connect with the Father.

Hebrew prophets earnestly desired to understand God's plan of salvation. They desired to understand how God would live with humanity and how He would deal with our sinful nature. Knowing the holy nature of God, they knew He could not co-exist with the brokenness of humanity unless there was a way to redeem the very nature of men. This was God's plan of salvation. He made a way to infuse Himself into every believer.

Though the message of salvation is easy to understand, the practical view of how it is evident in the life of a believer brings with it some challenging questions. Why does a believer who claims to have been transformed, seem to struggle with their pre-salvation identity? Living in the tension of a transforming identity draws much criticism as to when a believer is actually changed.

The question of who does or does not possess salvation has confounded sincere believers for centuries. However, the teachings of Jesus give us a clear standard by which we can evaluate our salvation and the evidence of salvation in others. Let's take a look at this topic in the next chapter.

Chapter 4
Evidence of Salvation

"It is not thy hold on Christ that saves thee; it is Christ. It is not thy joy in Christ that saves thee; it is Christ. It is not even thy faith in Christ, though that be the instrument; it is Christ's blood and merit."
- Charles Spurgeon

The Elder

He was a wife beater. Everyone knew it. He was an elder in the church, but his title proved to be the only merit he possessed. Known around town for his anger and shrewd business ethics, he looked out only for himself. He had no children, and his wife had escaped the shackles of his rage a few months before his path crossed mine. I was a guest speaker at his Sunday school class. Immediately after my host dismissed the class, this elder approached me with his disapproval.

With criticism on the Bible translation I used and of the other authors I had citied, he let me have it. He presented himself as the final authority on all things spiritual, and he was determined to convince me of it. He claimed to be a Christian, but many would have sooner believed he was a former Soviet dictator. He touted his years of financial contributions to the church as evidence of his devotion to God. He spouted off a few Scriptures to me before he dismissed the full content of my message. I smiled and mumbled a conciliatory "Thank you," as I walked away.

Driving home, I questioned whether men like him are truly saved. If they are, what are they saved from? Was I being too judgmental in expecting his behavior to reflect his claim of having a relationship with Jesus? It wasn't just a momentary meeting with this man that sparked my questions. This man had lived in his hardened state for years and he remains in it to this day. Is he saved? Some would say, "Of course not, just look at his life!" Others would claim "We really can't judge his heart."

The Professor

I was a few semesters into my college career when I found myself seated in his humanities class. He was the complaint of most college students. Within five minutes of meeting him, I knew why. He claimed to be a follower of Jesus, but everything about him demonstrated the contrary. His drug paraphernalia was a little less than humorous. The ease with which he discussed sexually explicit topics assaulted the conscience of even the most liberal student. He had no problem with yelling at students. He had no qualms about telling them how ignorant they were. I sat stunned for weeks before he set his crosshairs on me. I had no desire or preparation to debate him.

I didn't agree with most of his perspectives, but I avoided making eye contact in the hopes he would do the same; but my evasion didn't last long. One day after class as I walked past his desk and he blurted out, "I was once a preacher, you know?" I wasn't sure how to respond. "I believe in Jesus," He continued. "Really?" I asked. I didn't mean to vocalize my question, but it fumbled out. "Oh yes," he said. Then he began a monologue about how cultural norms are too restrictive and how the Church is nothing more than a bunch of hypocrites. The obvious contradiction of his own life seemed to escape his notice. I had two semesters with that professor, and all the while he claimed to be a follower of Jesus. No one dared to challenge him on this claim. No one really knew what to make of any of his incongruent claims. He was given a platform to speak into the lives of hundreds of students for Jesus. But it seems his primary concern was to coerce students into his pseudo-spiritual, self-indulging ideas.

During my final semester in that college, I wrote an editorial for the paper criticizing cults and deviant religious sects. The article was in the wake of the David Koresh siege in Waco, Texas (1993). In it I jokingly referenced how twisting theology, as my professor often did, can lead to real world problems—problems like newly emerging cults. After submitting my article for print, a quick phone call from the professor halted the press, and the article was removed. So much for freedom of the press on the college campus!

In retrospect I ask myself: Was he saved? Was he in a relationship with the same Jesus I knew? Could he have known the Living God and yet live in such a vulgar expression of life, sexuality and broken faith?

I've put myself under the same microscope, especially during the formative years of my faith. When I failed, I felt the weight of my sin burden my soul for days. The constant question of "Am I pleasing God?" evolved into doubts about my own salvation. I lived in doubt for years. The oft-proclaimed unconditional love of God seemed very conditional on my ability to be a good person. Almost every preacher I discussed my concerns with reinforced the notion that salvation, though it may have been free, can only be maintained at a great cost of being sinless. "Who is truly saved?" I would often wonder.

I write of these personal struggles because the questions "Who is saved?" and "Am I saved?" are frequently asked. These questions can be a source of much internal turmoil for Christians. Therefore, it is worthwhile to pause and explore in-depth what salvation truly is by looking at both Galatians and other relevant passages in Scripture.

Before we dive into a response, however, let me clarify the motive of my inquiry. If we question ones salvation with the desire to disqualify them because of their behavior, then it will only cause confusion and condemnation. However, if we look at how salvation is defined and demonstrated throughout the scriptures, we can gain a liberating view of the most powerful act any soul can experience.

Paul first emphasized how the Galatians were not saved by the keeping of outwardly visible traditions or behavior (Gal. 3:1-3). They were saved by the internal working of the Spirit. Then he goes on to explain what the indwelling of the Holy Spirit should look like in a believer's life (Galatians 5:22-23).

However, as we discussed in the previous chapter, the first element common to the accounts of salvation is faith. Each follower of Jesus began with a belief in Jesus' claim to be God. Their belief then produced a change in their lives. But for many there is a window of time between belief and significant habit changes. So, we must ask at what point is one actually "saved." To answer this, we can turn to the most insightful parable Jesus gave to His disciples.

The Farmer and Seeds

The context of Christ's story is an illustration of how one receives and maintains belief in what God has said. If belief in what God has said is necessary for salvation—identified as the "word"— this parable gives us insight into how one receives salvation and maintains it. Luke records the parable in this way:

And when a great multitude had gathered, and they had come to Him from every city, He spoke by a parable: A sower went out to sow his seed. And as he sowed, some fell by the wayside; and it was trampled down, and the birds of the air devoured it. Some fell on rock; and as soon as it sprang up, it withered away because it lacked moisture. And some fell among thorns, and the thorns sprang up with it and choked it. But others fell on good ground, sprang up, and yielded a crop a hundredfold. When He had said these things He cried, He who has ears to hear, let him hear!" (Luke 8:4-8 NKJV).

After the crowds dissipated, the disciples asked for insight into the parable, and Jesus explained the meaning of His story. He said,

Now the parable is this: The seed is the word of God. Those by the wayside are the ones who hear; then the devil comes and takes away the word out of their hearts, lest they should believe and be saved. But the ones on the rock are those who, when they hear, receive the word with joy; and these have no root, who believe for a while and in time of temptation fall away. Now the ones that fell among thorns are those who, when they have heard, go out and are choked with cares, riches, and pleasures of life, and bring no fruit to maturity. But the ones that fell on the good ground are those who, having heard the word with a noble and good heart, keep it and bear fruit with patience. (Luke 8:11-15 NKJV)

In Jesus' explanation, the seed represented the word of God. The phrase "word of God," as used in this passage, does not speak of a compiled Bible. How do we know this? First, because the Bible would not be produced in its full content until a few centuries later. There was no New Testament in existence. The first letter of the New Testament, Galatians, would not be written for years after this parable was spoken. Secondly, the Old Testament scriptures were not readily broadcast to a mass variation of recipients as the parable implies. In fact, only the highest of the religious leaders could access and read the scriptures. The third, and final, argument comes from God's desire to hold a conversational relationship with His people. In Exodus 19:5, God speaks to the Israelites saying, "If ye will obey my voice indeed, and keep my covenant, then ye shall be a peculiar treasure unto me above all people."[17] Even before the written text of the Pentateuch, God speaks to Israel of receiving and obeying His voice. A voice, by implication, which they could hear.

So, what does the "word of God" mean in this parable? The phrase is translated from the three Greek words "logos tou Theou." Here the meaning of *logos* or "word" is defined as "to speak or talk, to say, to tell."[18] *Logos* could include receiving a message through written text, but the Greek word *rhemati*, is more commonly used for a written message. For example, in Luke 4:4, *rhemati* strongly implies the written scriptures of the Old Testament. The words *logos* and *rhemati* could be interchanged but taking into consideration how this parable was passed on verbally, we can safely infer the more accurate meaning of logos is the spoken word.

---

17 The Holy Bible: King James Version. Electronic Edition of the 1900 Authorized Version. (Bellingham, WA: Logos Research Systems, Inc., 2009).
18 Eugene Nida and Johannes P. Louw. Greek-English Lexicon of the New Testament Based on Semantic Domains, Electronic ed. of the 2nd edition., Vol. 1. (New York: United Bible Societies, 1996), 396.

Why should we note the differences of these words as they are used in this parable? Because believers too often ignore the voice of God speaking in their thoughts and restrict His ability to communicate to designated times of Scripture reading. God does speak through scripture, but He also communicates with us by His Spirit who lives in us.

When Jesus talks about the word of God in His parable, the four responses he points out are not the reactions of people to scriptural text but to the hearing of God's voice. With a clearer understanding of what the seed symbolizes, we can evaluate Jesus' conclusions in this parable. This parable gives us a clear standard by which we can understand who is saved or in need of salvation.

The first group consists of those who heard God's voice but failed to believe God was speaking them. The members of this group are robbed by the enemy of the little revelation needed to receive salvation. Jesus tells us these hearers lose the seed to the "birds of the air" and do not believe. As a result, they are not saved (Luke 8:12). There is no confusion on this point. Hearers who are unresponsive to God's voice do not inherit eternal life.

The second group are those who hear God's voice and respond. They receive what they hear with a joyful attitude, but the word has "no root." Without reading too much into the analogy, we can safely equate rocky soil with those who make no room for God's words to affect them. God's word doesn't penetrate into the practical aspects of how they believe and subsequently live. They can hear God's word preached, taught and sung. They can even get excited about what they hear, but there is no lasting change.

Rocky soil indicates one who restricts Jesus' teachings to only metaphorical or positive messages which produce nothing more than a nod of acceptance. These, according to this text, believe for a while, but in the time of temptation they fall away. The phrase "fall away" in Luke 8:13 is actually one word in the original language. It is the word aphistantai, and it means "to remove," either spatially or from the context of a state or relationship. [19]

This same root word and context is used by Paul in his letters to Timothy. In 1 Timothy 4:1-2, Paul speaks of those who "depart from the faith" because they are deceived. In 2 Timothy 2:19, he uses this word to urge believers to "depart from" iniquity. In short, this separation from the faith doesn't indicate a temporal doubt, but it emphasizes the removal of oneself from a relationship with God. Such people choose to nullify the faith to which they once emotionally connected. As a consequence of this separation, this group is not counted among those who are saved.

The third group Jesus speaks of are those who received His word, but the seed falls among thorns. He says these heard God's voice, but they went out and were "choked with cares, riches, and pleasures of life" (Luke 8:14). As a result, this group "brought no fruit to maturity." Did this group at one point have a sincere faith which produced salvation? To bring a little more clarity to this idea we can look at another parable Jesus shared about those who are consumed with pleasure.

In Luke 12:42-48, Jesus tells of a servant who believed his master was delayed in returning to him. The servant said in his heart, "My lord delays his coming." Then he began to "beat the servants and maids, and to eat and drink, and to be drunken." Jesus concludes by

19 K. H. Rengstorf, G. Kittel, G. W. Bromiley, & G. Friedrich, eds. Theological Dictionary of the New Testament, electronic ed.(Grand Rapids, MI: Eerdmans, 1985).

saying, "the lord of that servant will come in a day when he is not looking for him, and at an hour when he is not aware, and will cut him in sunder, and will appoint him his portion with the unbelievers."

From this we can see the clear warning Jesus gives. Those who are preoccupied with personal pleasure will face His judgment and have their "portion with unbelievers." This means they will enter the same eternal judgement of those who did not believe. Jesus goes on to say that we are responsible for the knowledge of salvation we have been given. He says, "For everyone to whom much is given, from him much will be required; and to whom much has been committed, of him they will ask the more" (Luke 12:48).

In Matthew and Mark's account of this same parable of the sower, those who are consumed with the cares of life are declared to be "unfruitful" (Matthew 13:22, Mark 4:19). The Greek word for "unfruitful" (akarpos) can also be translated as "impiety, ungodliness, works of ungodliness; lusts or desires after evil things." The word "unfruitful" doesn't imply a small quantity of good character, but rather an excess of bad character. In conclusion, this group, according to the language of the text, appears to be unchanged and void of salvation.

The fourth and final group in this parable are those who hear God's voice and respond by continuously obeying it. The outcome is a fruit-producing life. Fruit, in this context, is defined as those "who show their knowledge of religion by their conduct." [20]

We can conclude from Jesus' parable that those who hear God's word and obey it reflect the evidence of God's Spirit in them by their lifestyle. This doesn't imply that there will be no struggles to live in

---

20 Thayer, J. H. A Greek-English lexicon of the New Testament: being Grimm's Wilke's Clavis Novi Testamenti. (New York: Harper & Brothers, 2010), 326.

the righteousness which God has put in them, but rather the evidence of a struggle will show God's nature producing a change. When someone claims to be an heir of salvation but regularly dismiss the voice of God and shows themselves to be consumed with the cares of life, this is a contradiction. When one is persistently distracted in their ability to hear God's voice because they make no opportunity for Him to affect them, they hold no evidence of salvation. Only those who hear God's voice and allow it to change them are heirs of salvation. Does this mean our behavior is the cause of salvation? No, behavior is merely the evidence of the salvation we have.

By Faith Alone

A common rebuttal to the teaching that one's faith must be evident in their behavior is the doctrine of "sola fide," interpreted as the teaching of "by faith alone." This understanding of salvation is attributed to the writings of the protestant reformer Martin Luther. The misunderstanding of his teachings has led into an unhealthy understanding of faith. Often faith is equated to a feeling or momentary belief in God. In this limited definition, one can separate believing in God from the behavior it should produce. When we expect behavior to reflect one's faith, the proponents of "by faith alone" rise to defend their position. They say that if we require godly behavior to be an indicator of salvation, we are perpetuating a works-based salvation. Can we, as believers, be foolish enough to think the mighty work of God's indwelling Spirit somehow will not cause a visible change?

In his book Spirit of the Discipline, Dallas Willard highlights Kierkegaard's criticism of the "faith alone" fallacy. He says,

"Kierkegaard's biting comments on how history has twisted Luther's teaching of salvation by faith express deep insight into our own situation today. He noted how there is always a certain worldliness that desires to seem Christian, but as cheaply as possible. This worldliness took note of Luther, listened closely to him, and found something it could make excellent use of. 'So, all comes by faith alone! Wonderful! We are free from all works. Long live Luther! Who loves not women, wine, and song remains a fool his whole life long!' This is the significance of the life of Luther, this man of God who, suited to the times, reformed Christianity." [21]

Willard and Kierkegaard both spoke to *the enticement of shallow faith which tends to lure the faint-hearted into a mediocre life.* We are saved by the grace of God and our response, as mentioned before, is an act of faith. This faith, however, is directly evident in the brave new life we lead. We are saved to be led by God's voice.

Accidental Eternal Life

A few years ago, a world-renowned celebrity passed away. He died tragically. His life was one of unbridled lust and lavish self-promotion. He had never made any statements which led any to consider him as one who held a concern for the eternal. A few weeks following his death, a televangelist declared how this celebrity could possibly be in Heaven. His argument was to emphasize the redeeming power of God's grace. He explained how in a moment of faith, this celebrity, as a child many years before, could have reached out to God. God in his goodness would have had no other choice but to welcome him into eternity. Really? Is this how grace and faith work? This is not grace, it is pure presumption. Yes, grace can be qualified as unmerited favor from God. However, the work of grace in us, after we receive it, draws out of us God's identity. Remember Paul's statement in Ephesians 2?

21 Willard, Dallas. The Spirit of the Disciplines (p. 39). HarperOne. Kindle Edition.

Ephesians 2:8-10

For by grace you have been saved through faith, and that not of yourselves; it is the gift of God, not of works, lest anyone should boast. For we are His workmanship, created in Christ Jesus for good works, which God prepared beforehand that we should walk in them.

Grace is given to us as we believe in the One who gives it. This resulting union of God's grace and our faith produces an identity in us which looks like Jesus. Our lives are redeemed to display the good works which God has prepared for us. Can one have faith and not have it reflected in their behavior? Martin Luther directly answers this in saying,

O, this faith is a living, busy, active, powerful thing! It is impossible that it should not be ceaselessly doing that which is good. It does not even ask whether good works should be done; but before the question can be asked, it has done them, and it is constantly engaged in doing them. But he who does not do such works, is a man without faith. He gropes and casts about him to find faith and good works, not knowing what either of them is, and yet prattles and idly multiplies words about faith and good works.

Luther continues to define of faith by saying,

[Faith] is a living well-founded confidence in the grace of God, so perfectly certain that it would die a thousand times rather than surrender its conviction. Such confidence and personal knowledge of divine grace makes its possessor joyful, bold, and full of warm affection toward God and all created things—all of which the Holy Spirit works in faith.

Hence, such a man becomes without constraint willing and eager to do good to everyone, to serve everyone, to suffer all manner of ills, in order to please and glorify God, who has shown toward him such grace.[22]

As we can see, the link between sincere faith and righteous behavior is undeniable, even in the writings of Martin Luther. Turning back to Christ's parable, Jesus tells the disciples about the fourth group who receive God's word. These hear God's voice and are transformed, producing a hundred-fold response. Others show a little less transformation. They produce a thirty-fold or a sixty-fold response. What could these three tiers of harvest mean? In light of the overall text, it would make sense to equate one's level of willingness to hear and obey to the thirty, sixty, and hundred-fold outcome. Jesus is showing us how God's voice can take root and impact the triune nature of our nature. The regenerating work of hearing God's voice has the ability to change us on the three levels of our identity.

Complete Salvation

Salvation is first spiritual. A believer is transformed from being a dead spirit bound in sin to being alive, in right relationship with God (Ephesians 2:1-10). Secondly, one's soul is changed. One is directed to put off the old nature and put on the new nature of Jesus as he or she daily hears and obeys the voice of God (Ephesians 4:24, Romans 12:2). This new nature shifts one's character from being self-focused, self-preserving to one which is giving, loving and self-sacrificing. Finally, one is physically changed. The believer's body, broken by sin and sickness, is regenerated by the life of God in them (Romans 6:10-11).

To illustrate this three-part work of salvation in its practicality, Paul draws his readers back to the account of the well-known

22 Quoted in Fosdick, Harry Emerson. Great Voices of the Reformation: An Anthology. (New York: Modern Library, 1954), 121–22.

patriarch Abraham. He was changed in spirit. He emerged from an idol-worshipping family to become one who was directed by the voice of God. His soul was transformed from a cowardly, dishonest merchant to the "father of many nations." Finally, his body and his wife's body were regenerated with life so they could bear children (see Romans 4:16-21). Let us turn our focus to Abraham to witness how this three-part transformation occurred.

Chapter 5
Abraham

"And Abraham believed in the Lord; and he counted it to him for
righteousness."
-Genesis 15:6

Abraham (1813 BC–1638 BC)
Galatians 3:6–4:7

The Middle Bronze Age was in full swing as a developing Sume-
rian culture took root in the valley of Mesopotamia (Modern-day
Iraq). Naraam-Sin, grandson to the warrior Nimrod, sat on the
throne as the last of the Akkadian kings. [23] As a devout worshipper of
Nanna, an ancient lunar deity, he completed the construction of two
city temples before claiming his divine right to rule. His first temple
was built in Ur, also known as Ur-Kasdim, the second, in Haran.
In this era, we find an extra-biblical mention of Terah, Abraham's
father. He was an idol merchant in the city of Ur. During his time in
this community, he had three sons: Abram, Haran, and Nahor.

Terah was the eighth descendant from Shem, Noah's son. Shem
was 98 years old when the flood waters receded. Then Shem lived
five hundred years after the birth of his first son Arphaxad (Genesis 11:11). This places Shem's age at 390, and Noah at 893 years old
when Abram was born. When Noah died, Abram was 57 years old

23 Berlyn, Patricia. Jewish Bible Quarterly Vol. 33, No. 2 (City: Publisher, 2005).

and Shem was 447 (Genesis 11:26, 11:32, Acts 7:4). Calculating from this, we know Shem was probably able to give Abram a first-hand account of the flood and possibly the history of humanity from creation to his father's life.

The Book of Jasher

In Sefer HaYashar, also known as the historical book of Jasher, we find a few legends concerning Abraham. The book of Jasher, as cited in Joshua 10:13, and 2 Samuel 1:18, is used as a reputable reference. We also find mention of it in the Talmud and in the writing of Josephus. [24]This ancient text was recovered in Naples, Italy in 1625. This book, however, is one of three by the same title. The newer publications are counterfeits of the original work; however, the earliest manuscript is believed to be authentic. From it we gain valuable insights into Abraham's life—facts which may have been commonly understood by the Apostle Paul and his Galatian readers.

The book of Jasher records, "Avram (Abram) knew YHWH (Jehovah), and he went in His ways and traditions of YHWH, and YHWH his Elohim was with him."[25] When Abram was forty-nine, his grandfather passed away. The following year he went to his father Terah's house. Terah was the "captain of the host of king Nimrod, and he followed strange gods."[26] There Abram asked his father if he knew who made the heavens and the earth. His father directed him to the gods which were sheltered in a room of their home.

Abram went to the room and saw twelve gods made of stone and wood. Abram felt that his father's worship of false gods was foolish. To test the power of the gods, he asked his mother to make a savory dish of food to appease them. Then he took the meal and placed it in the center of the room. Patiently watching, he observed that the gods

24 8-9
25 Ibid 72
26 Ibid

did not move, speak, or eat.

The next day, Abram thought to himself that his meal may not have been favorable enough for the idols. He returned to his mother and requested a better meal for them. Then taking the new dish from his mother, he laid it before them and awaited a response. Again, nothing happened. Then the Spirit of Yahweh came upon Abram, and he took a hatchet and destroyed all the idols but one—the largest one. He placed the incriminating weapon in its hands.

Upon discovering this, Terah ran to Abram and asked what he had done. Abram calmly replied that when he brought a meal to the idols, they all stretched out their hands for it, and the largest one was enraged at this. The great idol went and got a hatchet and destroyed all the others. Terah replied to Abram saying,

> Is there in these gods spirit, soul or power to do all thou hast told me? Are they not wood and stone, and have I not myself made them, and canst thou speak such lies, saying that the large god that was with them smote them? It is thou that didst place the hatchet in his hands, and then said he smote them all." [27] Abram answered his father, "How canst thou then serve these idols in whom there is no power to do anything? Can those idols in which thou trustest deliver thee? Can they hear thy prayers when thou callest upon them? Can they deliver thee from the hands of thy enemies, or will they fight thy battles for thee against thy enemies, that thou shouldst serve wood and stone which can neither speak nor hear? And now surely it is not good for thee nor for the sons of men that are connected with thee, to do these things; are you so silly, so foolish or so short of understanding that you

27 Ibid 76

will serve wood and stone, and do after this manner? And forget the Lord God who made heaven and earth, and who created you in the earth, and thereby bring a great evil upon your souls in this matter by serving stone and wood? [28]

Enraged, Terah reported Abram's behavior to King Nimrod. The king responded in anger and ordered Abram to be thrown into a fire. Terah, realizing the consequence of his betrayal, brought the son of his servant and presented him as Abram. The wisemen of the king uncovered his scheming, and the king called Terah out on his deception. Fearfully, Terah blamed his deception on Haran, Abram's older brother. The king furiously ordered Haran and Abram to be burned alive. Then, as the whole family watched, Abram and Haran were cast in the fire. Haran died, but Abram lived. He lived for three days in the fire because Yahweh was with him.

Taking this story into account, it is clear Abram believed YHWH to be God long before we find him in the book of Genesis. The Scriptures do not speak of Terah's conflict with Abram, but they begin with his northward journey from the land of Ur. They could have been traveling to Haran because it was the second city temple constructed by Nimrod. Being an idol merchant, it seems probable he would want to be near the newest temple site. When they reached what is known today as the southern border of Turkey, they stopped in a city ironically named after his recently deceased son, Haran.

Moses, in the Genesis account, confirms Haran's death by stating he died "in the presence (or face) of his father" Genesis 11:28 (KJV). Then, after Terah's death, YHWH spoke to Abram and directed him to leave his father's house. God promised to make him into a nation (Genesis 12:1-3). In response, Abram took with him Sarai as his wife

28 Ibid 76

and his brother Haran's son, Lot.

Abram was seventy-five years old when he began his journey. He arrived in Canaan and there built his first alter to God (Genesis 12:7-8). Moving further south, he encountered a famine in the land and continued into Egypt. Approaching the border of Egypt, he told his sixty-five-year-old wife that she was too beautiful. He feared the Egyptians will kill him to get her. To avoid this peril, he persuaded her to deceive the Egyptians and say she was his sister only. The Pharaoh's princes, as expected, noticed the beautiful Sarai and took her while Abram silently stood by. In an act of goodwill Pharaoh gave him oxen, donkeys, servants, and camels. Abram quietly accepted all these gifts.

Because Abram stood by passively, God stepped in and plagued Pharaoh's house. The Egyptians, who were strongly superstitious, connected the dots and drug Abram back to the palace to ask him why he had dealt so treacherously with them. He was then kicked out of Egypt with all his newly acquired wealth. Abram's cowardly betrayal of his wife to another man may indicate he didn't fully believe God' promise to him of a son. However, God was faithful to his promise and redeemed Abram out of his foolishness.

Traveling northward, Abram's assets increased, and the region he settled grew unable to support his expanding kingdom. Then Lot, his nephew, requested to separate from the growing caravan. Abram graciously gave Lot the first choice of territory and he eagerly selected the best place to settle. Then God spoke to Abram again and assured him that He would make him a great nation and his descendants will be innumerable. Abram was then directed to travel through the land (Genesis 13:14-18).

After this, war broke out among the nine kings in the region of the Jordan valley. In this war, Lot and his family were captured along with all the residents of Sodom. One escapee from the battle made it to Abram and reported the tragedy. Abram, showing a sign of self-sacrificing character, immediately assembled his army to raid one of the strongest military forces of his day. With a small troop of three hundred and eighteen, he rescued his nephew and all the captives of Sodom (Genesis 14:11-16).

When he returned victorious, Melchizedek, a possible pre-incarnate appearance of Jesus, visited him. In worship, Abram gave a tithe for the first and only recorded time to him. In response, Melchizedek pronounced a blessing over Abram (Genesis 14:18-20). This is another indicator of personal transformation in Abram's life. His generosity was noted as he worshipped God with a tenth of his possessions.

Then the king of Sodom attempted to reward Abram with material spoils of war, but Abram refused this gift. Note again how Abram, the coward who once took gifts from the Egyptians after lying to them, now refused gifts which could have been rightfully his. Why did he do this? He wanted to ensure the reason for his wealth was credited to his God and not to himself. In this we again see the soul of Abram maturing.

Then God appeared again to him in a vision, and Abram, having no offspring of his own at this time, suggested that perhaps Eliezer of Damascus, one of his servants, could be the heir of promise. Abram's soul was growing in the ability to be like the God he followed, but he struggled to believe in the promise given to him of a son to come. God replied to him that he would have a son.

In addition to this message, God reveals that his descendants will fall into slavery for four hundred years and afterward become great. To seal this prophesy, God made a covenant with him (Genesis 15:1-16). God caused Abram to fall into a deep sleep and then God passed between the cut pieces of Abram's sacrifice.

Then Abram's quest for a son took a little detour. Sarai offered Hagar to Abram so he could have a child by her. Abram complied, and Ishmael was born. Abram seemed to have no objections for all the obvious reasons of being offered a young woman, however, this silence on Abram's part could also indicate that he still didn't fully believe God's promise of a son through Sarai.

The situation, as expected, became contentious, and Abram allowed Hagar to be driven out from his camp (Genesis 16:1-6). God stepped in and consoled Hagar and foretold the secure future of her son. His name, given by the angel of the Lord, was Ishmael. After this, Hagar and Ishmael returned to Abram's camp. About this time, Abram was ninety-nine years old.

God appeared to him again and changed his name to Abraham and Sarai's name to Sarah. During this event God presented the covenant of circumcision (Genesis 17:1-11). Abraham again futilely attempted to make Ishmael the child of promise, but God objected. He assured Abram that Ishmael's future would be great, however, he would not the promised son (Genesis 17:18-21).

God made a final affirmation with Abram of His covenant when He went to discuss the issues within the cities of Sodom and Gomorrah (Genesis 18:9). Concerned for his nephew Lot, Abraham negotiated with God for these cities. The angels of the Lord visited Sodom and extracted Lot and his family before it was burned to the ground.

A few months passed, and Abraham headed south to find himself resorting to an old pattern of deception with Abimelech (another Pharaoh).[29] He and Sarah conspired to lie to Abimelech regarding their relationship. Abraham again feared being slain for the sake of Sarah (Genesis 20:1-17). After being told that she was only Abraham's sister, Abimelech took Sarah as his wife. Again, God stepped in to correct Abraham's folly. Sarah was returned to Abraham, and they continue on.

Finally, after many years of wavering between strong faith and faltering in belief, Abraham and Sarah received the healing power of God into their own bodies and Sarah conceived and gave Abraham his promised son, Isaac (Genesis 21:1-8). In the time from God's promise to the birth of Isaac, we see Abram mature from a caravanning merchant to a father of faith.

We can see how zealous he was for God; however, his behavior was minimally moral at best. He tithed once, sacrificed a handful of times, lied frequently, and looked for ways to fulfill his desire for a son on two occasions in direct contradiction to the promise God gave him. However, Abraham's final near-sacrifice of his only son, which God initiated to test him, stands as a profound act of faith. By the end of the story, Abraham was confident in God's promise of his descendants to come. He believed God could give him an heir even if He had to raise his son from the dead (Hebrews 11:19).

This is Paul's emphatic point. Abraham performed no great feats of holiness to acquire the given righteous identity God proclaimed over him. He simply believed God's promise to him. His belief pro-

29 Mackey, Damien F.. "Menes and Naram-Sin", JEA 6, no. 2, (April 1920): 89-98.

gressively transformed him in spirit, soul, and body.

Paul eloquently stated that Abraham, at the age of ninety-nine, "staggered not at the promise" (Romans 4:20). He went on to say that his example is given to show us how righteousness, or God's divine identity, can also be credited to us who believe with persistent faith. When we allow God's voice to speak to us, as He did to Abraham, we can be changed in our own spirit, soul, and body. We can see God hinting at this reality of His indwelling grace in the way in which God changed the name of Abraham, giving him a new beginning.

What's In A Name?

I want to insert an overlooked revelation about Abram and Sarai's transformation at the moment God made a covenant with them. When God appeared to Abram at ninety-nine years old, He changed Abram's and Sarai's names. This change was a promise not only to them but also to show all of humanity how God would insert His righteous identity into men and women.

Torah teachers believe Yahweh took the two "H" sounds from His name and placed them into Abraham & Sarah's names. "God's name consists of four Hebrew letters: yod, hei, vav, hei. Note how the letter hei is used twice. In keeping with the covenant, God added the letter hei to Abram's name, making it Abraham. He also added the letter hei to Sarai's name, making it Sarah. In other words, God gave them half of His own Name.[30]

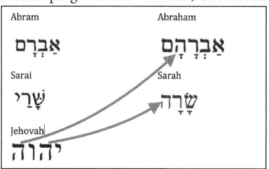

30 http://torahmatters.blogspot.com/2016/09/genesis-15-blood-covenant.html

The added hei is also the fifth letter of the Hebrew alphabet, and it carries a profound meaning. Hei is made of two parts: the dalet and yud. The dalet is the horizontal line (signifying width) and a connected vertical line (signifying height); these together represent the material world. The yud (the detached left leg) represents God.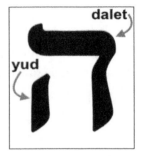

In this imagery, Torah scholars interpret the strokes to represent God (signified by the yud) entering into the material world of man (signified by the dalet). [31] In essence, God didn't simply change Abram's name; He added to his name the image of Himself living within Abram and Sarai. This would be a possibility after men and women would be made worthy of God's indwelling Spirit. The letter hei, as the fifth letter of the Hebrew alphabet, also signifies grace. In a literary sense, we could say God inserted grace from His name or identity into Abram and Sarai.

This grammatical word picture is an image of how God would infuse His righteous nature into every believer. Just as God placed a part of his name into Abraham's name, so He inserts His very Spirit into the consciousness of every believer.

31 https://www.chabad.org/library/article_cdo/aid/137077/jewish/Heh.htm#footnote1a137077

Chapter 6
Righteous Identity and the Law

"The righteousness of Jesus Christ is one of those great mysteries, which the angels desire to look into, and seems to be one of the first lessons that God taught men after the fall."
- George Whitefield

We've now seen how God led Abraham into his righteous identity. Through the years of Abraham's faith in God's promise, he was changed. In view of this, Paul says,

> Therefore, know that only those who are of faith are sons of Abraham. And the Scripture, foreseeing that God would justify the Gentiles by faith, preached the gospel to Abraham beforehand, saying, "In you all the nations shall be blessed." So then those who are of faith are blessed with believing Abraham (Galatians 3:8-9).

God promised Abraham a nation would be born from his lineage. This promise, as he held on to it, changed him. His identity developed into one who was called, "a friend of God" (James 2:23). Abraham's son and grandsons looked forward to God fulfilling His promise. The promise, however, was more than a lineage of descendants. It was a promise of a Savior to come who would deliver them from the evils of humanity (Genesis 22:18). The evil, though often perceived by the Hebrews as hostile invading armies, ran deeper in the veins of all humanity.

How could the Jews overcome the evil within themselves? God's plan all along was for them to listen to His voice and allow their obedience to cultivate in them His righteous nature. Because men and women could not obey God's voice, the moral law was given to convert unrighteous men into God's righteous nature (1 Timothy 1:9). But there was and still remains a significant problem. The hearts of men are inclined toward selfishness.

This self-serving propensity is directly opposed to the nature of God. God, in his mercy gave the moral law to Moses. However, this law only confirmed the internal moral law God had written into the heart of every human (Romans 2:15). Regardless of how men learned right from wrong, whether by their conscience or by the understanding of God's written law, only one conclusion transpired. No matter how moral we desire to be, we don't have the ability to sustain the righteous identity necessary for relationship with God.

What then is the solution? A compete identity change. This is why Paul says, "For you are all sons of God through faith in Christ Jesus" (Gal. 3:26). Why does the idea of being a son emerge? Because it was God's plan all along. We were created to be God's offspring, fully infused with His righteous identity.

We read of many glimpses of this hope throughout the scriptures (Acts 17:29, Psalms 82:1-6, John 10:34-35). From the lineage, in which see Abraham arise, we see continual examples of men and women who carried on the successive lineage as descendants of God. This is why the monotonous list of one man begetting of another is so vital to the scriptural records (Matthew 1:1-17, Luke 3:23-38). The Hebrews successfully traced their roots back to God Himself. This is why the historian Luke traces the genealogy of Jesus back to Adam. He poignantly concludes his narrative with ". . . Seth, the son of Adam, the son of God" (Luke 3:38).

God's intent has always been for us to be in His family. Adam and Eve were given the place of honor as the "son of God" (This title applied to both Adam and Eve). As God's children, they lived in perfect union with the Father, but when that relationship was broken, their godlikeness was lost. Adam and Eve had been created with a sinless nature; righteousness was their default way of thinking and behaving.

We can understand this "default righteousness" through the example of a family. Families are known to share superficial attributes such as accents, facial expressions, or physical qualities. Deeper attributes such as academic excellence, artistic abilities, or even skills can also define a family. Woven into all these inherited attributes is an inherited way of thinking. This belief system serves to be the framework for each person's perception of reality.

In this context, righteousness is the framework by which God thinks and behaves. As a result, those in His family must also possess the righteous nature. As King David writes, "Righteousness and justice are the foundation of Your throne" (Psalm 89:14). If God acted contrary to His nature, one could only imagine how utter chaos would overthrow the spiritual and natural world. When Adam and Eve, as God's children, acted outside of their righteous nature, evil entered into their being and the entire natural world was broken. Their realm of existence was delivered to the enemy (see Luke 4:6).

The first consequence Adam and Eve both experienced was an immediate sentence of physical death. Their bodies were created to exist forever, but as a result of sin, death began its corrupting work (Romans 5:12). Some Rabbinical authorities go so far to say, "Adam and Eve had their garments of celestial light replaced by 'garments of skin,' which merely protected but no longer illuminated."

The second consequence Adam and Eve's sin produced was a broken unity with God. This is the spiritual death that is referenced throughout Scripture (Ephesians 2:1, Ephesians 2:5, Colossians 2:13). Adam aimed his accusations at God and blamed Him for his disobedience. In other words, he lost his ability to be unified in thought with God. Their inability to perceive Him correctly began at this point. Jesus, however, did possess this unity and modeled how we can be restored to oneness with the Father (John 10:30, 17:22). The concept of reunification with God in our very consciousness is an underlying truth in John's Gospel and in his letters to the early Church. John calls this reunification "abiding in Christ" (John 14:16, 15:4, 6, 7, 10; 1 John 2:24, 27-28, 3:15).

The third consequence Adam and Eve's sin produced was a wounded soul. Their affections immediately turned inward rather than toward each other. Adam and Eve lost their ability to live in self-sacrificing love for each other. Their mind, will, and emotions defaulted to self-worship; they became their own gods.

The human body, spirit, and soul were infected by Adam and Eve's disobedience. Within a few generations, violence, sexual perversion, and pride poisoned all but one man's family —Noah, the preacher of righteousness (Genesis 6:5, 2 Peter 2:5-9). Peter's use of the word "righteousness" to compare Noah and Lot (Abrahams' nephew) to cultures of unrighteousness gives us insight into how deficient it was in the ancient world. Men lacked the righteous nature needed for a relationship with God. Shortly after Noah's flood had subsided (2348 B.C.), mankind became corrupt once more, and God's judgement was played out in the dispersion of civilization at the tower of Babel (2246 B.C.).

Then, 755 years later, God spoke to Israel in an attempt to rebuild His relationship with the Hebrews in the desert of Sinai. The Ten Commandments were given to Israel to bring an awareness of their need for Gods' righteous nature in them.

God revealed His desire to place His nature into Israel when He gave the Law to Moses. Later, in his address to Joshua, God desired for the Law to become Israel's way of thinking. He said to him, "This Book of the Law shall not depart from your mouth, but you shall meditate in it day and night, that you may observe to do according to all that is written in it. For then you will make your way prosperous, and then you will have good success" (Joshua 1:8).

The word "Law" in this verse can be defined as the "custom" or "manner" God directed Israel to follow.[32] Looking closer at the Law, we can gain a few insights that will clarify another reason Paul would present the Law to his non-Jewish audience. The Law gave us a glimpse into the essence of God's personality.

In giving the Law to Moses, God began by saying, "I am the Lord..." (Exodus 20:2). The importance of this proclamation goes

---

32 Strong, J. Enhanced Strong's Lexicon. (Woodside Bible Fellowship, 1995)

beyond an introductory phrase. God is communicating His moral requirements for His people, with His own character as the full embodiment of the principles He would dictate. The first four commandments state,

> You shall have no other gods before Me.
> You shall not make for yourself a carved image.
> You shall not take the name of the Lord your God in vain.
> Remember the Sabbath day. (Exodus 20:3-8)

These commandments speak to the way in which Israel, and by virtue every believer, can relate to God. He alone wants our affections and will not allow our devotion to be shared with any other being. He will not even allow a false view of Him—whether in our imagination or in the way we address Him—to blind us from who He is. God requires the use of His name to be spoken with honor and reverence. To authentically know and portray God is the key to producing a culture of acceptable behavior toward God. God even commanded our calendars to reflect a singular devotion to Him at the beginning of each week.

Jesus later clarifies the heart of God in these first four commands by citing Deuteronomy 6:4: "You shall love the Lord your God with all your heart, with all your soul, and with all your mind" (Matt. 22:37). This statement, known to the Jews as part of the Shema Yisrael prayer, highlights love as the driving force behind the commandments. God gave us the Ten Commandments to stir within us the longing to be like Him, not to merely enforce obedience (1 Timothy 1:5). Jesus then sums up the remaining six commands with the text from Leviticus 19:18: "You shall love your neighbor as yourself."

In these last six commands, God addresses our behavior toward others. From our relationship with our parents, to our neighbor, to the general public, these boundaries serve to show how God desires to work through us toward others. The purpose of the Ten Commandments is to cultivate a God-like character in the life of every follower. But as noted by many scholars, the law only speaks to the need we have for this right nature; it does not empower us to actually be righteous. It does not give us the ability to love God with all our being and to love others as ourselves.

Since the fall of Adam and Eve, God designed a plan to infuse His right nature back into our imperfect nature. His desire for us to fully inherit His qualities was revealed again and again to the Old Testament prophets (Deuteronomy 30:6; Ezekial 11:19-20, 18:31; Psalm 51:10, 36:26; Jeremiah 24:7, 31:33, 32:39; Joel 2:28). This plan and desire were fulfilled in Jesus.

As we turn to the New Testament, the word righteousness (dikaiosynen), as used by the apostle Paul, is defined as "the norm in the affairs of the world to which men and things should conform and by which they can be measured."[33] Just as the law was a legible, external ordinance of behavior set before the Jews, so the righteousness of God is an internal, Spirit-led awareness set within the believer. The atonement Jesus provides is not only a remedy for man's sin, but it also abolishes the Law that produces condemnation (Eph. 2:15). Paul emphasized this truth in his letter to the Colossians when he wrote,

And you, being dead in your trespasses and the uncircumcision of your flesh, He has made alive together with Him, having forgiven you all trespasses, having wiped out the handwriting of requirements that was against us, which was contrary to us. And He has taken it

33 Ladd, George Eldon. A Theology of the New Testament (Grand Rapids, MI: Eerdman's Publishing Company, 1974), 440-441.

out of the way, having nailed it to the cross (Colossians 2:13-14).

What does this mean for us today? It simplifies our salvation to a relationship with God. We no longer need to pursue the keeping of a moral law to attain a righteous nature. God has put His nature in us, and we need only believe He is in us. In this belief, we can simply follow His lead. As Paul would later say in his letter to the Romans, "as many as are led by the Spirit of God, these are sons of God" (Rom. 8:14).

In contradiction to this, we often hear religious leaders of our day prescribe a set of rules to new believers. This cumbersome mindset is taught with underlying fears of eternal condemnation if the laws of God are broken. We've all heard the conditional religious jargon that stokes the fire of condemnation in our soul. "If you love Jesus, then you'll _____." Fill in the blank. Sincere leaders offer this line of reasoning to encourage healthy habits, but often they inadvertently urge good behavior to be a necessity of maintaining one's salvation.

On the contrary, godly behavior should simply be the result of our transformation and the outworking of the salvation we possess. This is why Paul says in his letter to the Philippians, "...work out your own salvation with fear and trembling; for it is God who works in you both to will and to do for His good pleasure" (Philippians 2:12-13). The word work *katergazomai* in this text means, "to cause a state to be."[34] This means inside the believer is the righteous nature of God working to "will and to do His pleasure." They merely need to let it happen.

In our relationship with Jesus, our desire to express our love for Him is naturally communicated in our willingness to obey His voice

34 Louw, J. P., & Nida, E. A. (1996). Greek-English lexicon of the New Testament: based on semantic domains (electronic ed. of the 2nd edition., Vol. 1, p. 149). New York: United Bible Societies.

in us. Jesus did not abolish the moral law to provide a way for us to live lawlessly. No, He did away with sin and the law so we could live freely in love with Him. The result of this love is that we, by the power of the Holy Spirit, keep the law without consciously rehearsing it in our minds. The infusion of God's right nature into our own can possibly understood to be a partial transplant of His identity into our own.

Transplant Miracle

Our usual meeting spot was the Starbucks by the hospital. My good friend Eric and I had a pow-wow every week or so to talk about family, medicine and Christian apologetics. Our discussion a few weeks ago veered down an intriguing bunny trail. He told me about heart transplant patients who believed they had inherited unique traits from their donors.

In searching out a few medical magazines, I found a few articles that termed this transferring phenomenon as "cellular memory." A significant number of organ recipients felt a slight change in their personality after receiving a transplant. Although these studies were not fully accepted without criticism, their implications are intriguing. What if the cellular makeup of a vital organ carried with it the attributes of the donor? In these studies, 6%-15% of patients claimed to have noticed personality changes. Traits such as new eating habits, artistic skills, and other nuances emerged in the patients after their transplants.

In a more substantial way, the new Spirit we have transplanted into us makes alive our supernatural personality (Romans 8:11). God's nature in us is evidenced by one great attribute: just as Jesus lived in love with His Father and received the Father's love, we also are pulled into this place of love (John 15:9-11). We will have a love for the Father, and it will result in a desire to keep His commands. In fact, John, in his letter to the church, uses this love relationship between the Father and the Son as a litmus test for one's salvation (1 John 2:22-24).

This affection for the Father is transferred to us as children of God. The keeping of God's commands is the anticipated side effect of His heart being transplanted into us. This transplant occurs immediately in our acceptance of His salvation, but our "personality change" is progressive as we realize who we are in the person of Jesus. *This means the more insight or revelation we gain about Jesus, the more we are learning about who we are in Him.* This progressive revelation continues until we are fully redeemed.

On the day of our full redemption, we will look like, or behave like, Jesus (1 John 3:2). Paul poetically paints an image of this transformation in his famous statement, "For now we see in a mirror, dimly, but then face to face. Now I know in part, but then I shall know just as I also am known" (1 Corinthians 13:12).

To understand our need for the Law and a righteous nature, we may have to dig a little deeper into reason for our need to be righteous. Our desire to be like God in our identity stems from our soul's need for a father. Yes, it comes down to a family connection. We are all God's children looking for the overwhelming approval of our Father in Heaven.

Chapter 7
Father Hunger

"The greatest danger for a child, where religion is concerned, is not that his father or teacher should be an unbeliever, not even his being a hypocrite. No, the danger lies in their being pious and Godfearing, and in the child being convinced thereof, but that he should nevertheless notice that deep within there lies hidden a terrible unrest. The danger is that the child is provoked to draw a conclusion about God, that God is not infinite love."
- Søren Kierkegaard

During my early years in the ministry, I did what most youth pastors do. I took any job available to help fund my dreams of ministry. I worked at McDonald's, then at Walmart, then as a lab tech for an allergy clinic and then with a home builder. After these part-time jobs, I returned to college to finish my degree. After graduation, I took a job in the banking industry which led to various sales jobs.

While climbing this corporate ladder, I continued to serve as a youth pastor. Finally, I became a sales representative for a pharmaceutical company, and I felt I had financially arrived. I jokingly tell friends I went from selling mutual funds to selling cell phones, to selling drugs. I eagerly climbed the corporate ladder but struggled to fulfill the calling I knew I had on my life.By this time, I was married to my beautiful wife and we were both becoming aware of a deep deficit in my soul. Something was missing, but I didn't have a clue as to what it was.

Then a revelation moment happened. I was 26 years old and standing on the second-floor balcony of a popular club in Las Vegas. I was working for a pharmaceutical company and attending our annual sales meeting. That evening was to be the crowning night of the weekend.

Scanning the crowded floor, I noted my co-workers were having a great time, but my soul was empty. I was out of place. I felt like I had strayed far from the path of my Divine calling. I wasn't doing anything wrong, but my definition of success had changed, and I was uneasy with the life I had created. "Maybe I need to go into fulltime ministry and give up this career," I thought to myself. That thought kept playing over and over in my mind.

When I returned home, I shared my heart with my wife. She cried and amidst the tears, she objected, saying, "I don't want to be poor!" She had always supported my career ideas, but this one was a hard one to swallow. After consoling her with the financial plans I had been working on to make this transition, we made the jump. I went to our pastor at the time and told him our desire. He hesitantly agreed, and I resigned from my job and took a forty percent cut in pay to go into fulltime ministry.

Looking back, I'm sure this was the dumbest financial decision I have ever made. A year into our job as fulltime youth pastors our finances grew tight, and we were expecting our first son. In the next five years, we took three significant pay cuts, and our workload at the church continuously increased. As our senior pastor was battling cancer, we worked ceaselessly to aid the church's welfare. My wife faithfully encouraged me as we cultivated a youth ministry, birthed a college ministry and started a small business.

From Sunday morning sermons, to leading worship, to discipling small group leaders, to making hospital visits and conducting weddings and funerals, the responsibilities compounded. Ministry activities began to push out of my soul an awareness of my emotional needs. In all the busyness, I was looking for something. The something I was searching found me in the most barren of places.

February 2004

The North African heat seeped through every possible crack of the small concert-walled room. I lay pitifully on my back with my head throbbing and limbs aching. I didn't have time for a fever. It was the second day of our two-week mission. It took our team over twenty hours of flight jumping and bus driving to arrive at our missionary's house. Along the way I must have caught something. I felt my strength draining and my fever climbing. There was no nearby pharmacy. No doctors we could call. We only had our friendly missionaries who assured me that I should drink plenty of fluids, then led the team out for the morning.

Needless to say, a little panic set in, and I turned my frustration upward. "God," I said out loud, "I'm out here in the desert, thousands of miles from home. I came here to minister with our missionaries. You think You could help me out a little? It would be easy for You to heal me, so what's the problem?"

The pain seemed to increase as I tried to sit up and move around.

I stood up and realized I couldn't do much more without waves of nausea pushing me down. I crawled back under the thin sheets. Tears rolled down my face. I felt abandoned.

"Why don't you help me?" I whispered.

The throbbing intensified. "Why don't You help?"

As my fever spiked, I felt my mind frantically trying to make sense of where I was and what I was doing. I didn't know what else to do but lay still and wait. I didn't feel very spiritual. As I soaked the bed with sweat, I faded in and out of sleep.

"I Am not who you think I Am."

His voice came with an authoritative tone into my thoughts. I had heard Him clearly like that before, but not with this stern Fatherly tone.

"Who are you?" I asked in a fog of confusion.

Thoughts of a harsh God punishing me for some unknown sins came into my mind. "Why can't you heal me?" I asked again.

"Why are you here?" He responded.

"Why am I here? Don't You know?" I replied. "I'm out here to do Your work, but I'm sick in this bed because You won't help."

Childhood memories of being alone raced through my thoughts. As each one played, I felt a crippling stab of abandonment. "I am out here," I thought to myself, "because this is all I know to do. I don't know why I am here. Didn't You tell me to come here?"

Silence.

"What am I missing?"

"I Am the God of your father," He said.

"Father." That single word was a difficult image to process. I hated my dad. In my twenty-something years of life, my dad had merited little respect from me and, truth be told, I was probably his greatest frustration. I had no relationship with him, and the very hope of one caused too much pain.

"You cannot see me through the lens of your father," God continued. "You must see your father through Me."

His words peeled back my blindness. All the anger and sense of abandonment I had directed at God because of my dad fell off my eyes. The face of my dad was washed off the image of God in my soul. I looked through God's eternal eyes and saw the acceptance every child wants from their father. Unconditional love. It flooded my soul and filled my deep longing for approval. The hope of Divine connection replaced my sense of legalistic obligation toward God.

"Could God really be this good?" I wondered. I sat up and placed my hands on my soaked forehead. My brow was cool to the touch, and not a twinge of pain was left. I was completely healed. From that moment on, my soul began experiencing the Father in a powerful and healing way. The assurance of His acceptance began to change the lens through which I perceived my myself and the life I had before me.

This longing for a father's approval lays dormant in every soul. The brokenness and busyness of our culture, now more than ever, pushes to the surface hidden father wounds. In William Young's book The Shack, he identifies this unique father wound in every soul.

In the story, Mac raises a question to God, saying, "why is there such an emphasis on you being a Father? I mean, it seems to be the way you most reveal yourself."[35] God responds to Mac, saying, "There are many reasons for that, and some of them go very deep. Let me say for now that We knew once the Creation was broken, true fathering would be much more lacking than mothering… an emphasis on fathering is necessary because of the enormity of its absence."[36]

When the Father's voice spoke healing power into my broken body that day, His love penetrated to the deep-seated wound in my soul. That wound, though it is experienced in different ways by each of us, is God's primary concern. He is looking to his family. His passion is to reconcile the entire world back into a relationship with Himself (2 Corinthians 5:19).

Applying God's healing balm, Paul writes a liberating truth in Galatians 4:4-7. He says, Jesus came "…that (you) might receive the adoption as sons. And because you are sons, God has sent forth the Spirit of His Son into your hearts, crying out, 'Abba, Father!' Therefore, you are no longer a slave but a son, and if a son, then an heir of God through Christ."

This right nature we desire is an expression of a deep-seated de-

35 Young, William P.. The Shack (p. 95). Windblown Media.
36 Ibid

sire to gain the approval of our Father. This longing is a hope to possess a right-nature before our Father. We long for His approving nod. We hope for unconditional acceptance. This desire may have driven you to perform for God's approval in the past, but the good news is that we are made sons in salvation. You can be born into unwavering approval! When you realize you are in right-standing with the Father from the day of your salvation, you will discover liberation from the lie that you need to do something more to gain God's acceptance.

The Big Lie

One last thought. As we addressed the origin of humanity as God's children in the previous chapter, consider how the enemy, in the form of a snake, began his deception with Eve. He seeded doubt in her mind saying, "God knows that in the day you eat of it (the fruit) your eyes will be opened, and you will be like God..."[37] The temptation was not merely to eat a forbidden fruit, it was to believe she could be like God. God was holding out on her.

This was the big lie. It is the same lie the enemy perpetuates in the mind of every believer. With a little twist, and cunning slither, he creeps into our thoughts and begins to tell us we are not like God in our nature. "You are not righteous," he says. "But if you truly want to be like God, then you'll read your Bible more. You would pray much more. You wouldn't be so easily angered." With every challenge to the righteous nature you have within you, another link is forged in the chain of self-condemnation.

Many who are bound to the lies of the enemy view their relationship with Jesus as journey from one failure to the next. The truth, however, is the same with us as it was with Adam and Eve. They were more like God than anyone else in creation spanning from their time

37 The New King James Version. (1982). (Ge 3:5). Nashville: Thomas Nelson.

to the arrival of Jesus.

The same is true for you. Inside you, the full nature of God has been deposited and the power of sin has been destroyed. The more you believe you possess the right nature of God in you, the easier it becomes to manifest God's identity in your daily life. As a follower of Jesus there is nothing more God can do for you to pull you closer to Him. You need only to believe and allow this belief to become the guiding thought in your mind. You belong to your Father and you have the identity of your Father placed in you.

How does this right nature lifestyle come into existence? One day at a time. It manifests through the regular practice of being with your Father. Each of us, whether intentionally or not, see God through the lens of our earthly fathers. For some this is a positive view. For others, much pain and disillusionment occur when they think about God as a father.

In his exhaustive work, *Faith of the Fatherless: The Psychology of Atheism,* Dr. Paul C. Vitz points to his irrefutable research which highlighted this truth. In his study, Vitz shows how the giants of atheism such as Fredrich Nietzche, David Hume, Bertrand Russell, Jean-Paul Sartre, Albert Camus, Richard Dawkins, Christopher Hitchens and many more had the common heritage of an absent or abusive father. He contrasts this by showing how his control group of thinkers such as Blaise Pascal, George Berkeley, William Wilberforce, Alexis de Tocquville, Edmund Burke, G.K. Chesterton, Dietrich Bonhoeffer and many more had healthy fathers and a consequently healthy view of God. Whether you want to admit it or not, the lens through which you perceive God is significantly clouded by the influence of your earthly father.

In chapter ten of his book *Boundaries,* Dr. Henry Cloud clearly identifies how a healthy relationship with a parent can translate into a healthy view of God and subsequently all authority a child will grow to face. I highlight these two books because they are written by renown psychologists who have sufficiently linked one's perception and response to God to be closely tied to their response to an earthly father. Knowing this, you may consider the following questions to discover how your view of God may be influenced or distorted by your own father.

- In what ways did you try to gain your father's (or parents) approval as a child?
- Do you feel you were successful in getting approval?
- In what ways do you feel you are trying to get God's approval?
- Have you possibly made a set of rules in your mind to follow in hopes for God's approval?
- Can you believe you have God's approval?

Read the following passages of Scripture and write how God feels about you. Ephesians 1:5-6, Colossians 1:13, Romans 5:5.

Prayer: *Father, I want to be close to you and experience the love You have for me. I confess I've been trying to gain your approval by _____ (list the good or bad behaviors you've allowed into your life.) I receive Your righteousness. I receive Your righteous identity in me. Lead me by Your Spirit. Open my thoughts to hear Your voice like a son/ daughter. Amen.*

Chapter 8
One Law to Obey

"Love recognizes no barriers. It jumps hurdles, leaps fences, penetrates walls to arrive at its destination full of hope."
– Maya Angelou

The Law places a demand on each person to replicate God's righteous nature. With this precondition to a healthy relationship with God, it is evident how the transplant of Jesus' righteous nature into us is the only hope we have. So, what happens after we accept God's righteous nature into our life? Is that the end of our quest? Yes, we are made righteous, but the work of salvation is not merely a connection with God. The realization of our righteous nature should have an affect outside of our relationship with God. It must permeate our relationships with others. This expectation falls into the greater purpose God desired for humanity.

God spoke his intent to Adam and Eve when he said, "Be fruitful and multiply; fill the earth and subdue it…" (Genesis 1:28). God always planned for mankind to transfer His righteous identity from one generation to the next (Deuteronomy 6:6-7). God's passion for generational progression of righteousness is shown in His reason for selecting Abraham. He says in Genesis 18:19 (ESV), "For I have chosen him (Abraham), that he may command his children and his household after him..." (Genesis 18:19).

This transfer of our righteous nature is also echoed by Asaph, the popular lead musician of King David. In Psalms 78:5–7 he says,

> For He (God) established a testimony in Jacob,
> And appointed a law in Israel,
> Which He commanded our fathers,
> That they should make them known to their children;
> That the generation to come might know them,
> The children who would be born,
> That they may arise and declare them to their children,
> That they may set their hope in God,
> And not forget the works of God,
> But keep His commandments;

Not only does God desire for us to walk in His right nature for the benefit of those we love, but we carry His nature for a world which has lost sight of His true essence. This point is highlighted throughout the New Testament letters. They emphasized how we are to allow the identity of God shine out of us (Matthew 5:16; John 1:8, Romans 12:9, 1 Peter 2:12).

The right nature given to us is not to empower self–righteousness. Rather, we are given this identity in Jesus for the sake of communicating the hope everyone has of being a son or daughter of God. We are saved to save. Paul, in his letter to the Corinthians says,

> Now all things are of God, who has reconciled us to Himself through Jesus Christ, and has given us the ministry of reconciliation, that is, that God was in Christ reconciling the

world to Himself, not imputing their trespasses to them, and has committed to us the word of reconciliation. Now then, we are ambassadors for Christ, as though God were pleading through us: we implore you on Christ's behalf, be reconciled to God. For He made Him who knew no sin to be sin for us, that we might become the righteousness of God in Him (1 Corinthians 5:18-21).

Here it is again, the fullness of the gospel message said in a simple way. God made Jesus to be sin for us so we could possess the right nature. This right nature is to aid us in the task of reconciling others to God. We are commissioned from the day of our salvation to relay the message of salvation to all who are held captive by the lie of not being good enough for relationship with our Father.

Down to One Rule

In the New Testament Jesus summarizes the moral law and all of its implications into two laws: Love God and love your neighbor (Matthew 22:37–40). The way we connect in devotion with God is secured by Jesus' death and resurrection. When we receive the indwelling Spirit of God by faith in Christ's work on the cross, God places Himself in us. He puts in us an ability to love and know Him (Galatians 4:6-7, Romans 5:5, Romans 8:15-16, John 8:42). His atonement implanted the righteousness He requires into us.

Remember when we receive the Holy Spirit, our righteous behavior is affirmed not by our ability to be moral, but rather through believing and obeying what we hear from God. As the well-known decree of the Protestant Reformation emphasized, "The just shall live by faith" (Romans 1:17). If the first of Jesus' two commands is met by His own work of atonement, then what is left for us to do? Paul answers this question with a liberating directive to the Galatian church. He says, "For all the law is fulfilled in one word, even in this: 'You shall love your neighbor as yourself'" (Galatians 5:14).

How we love others is the manifestation of the righteousness God has placed in us. I cannot emphasize this point enough. We are the image of God to fellow believers and to unbelievers. God's most significant concern is that we reflect His image well. We see this thought reinforced in numerous passages throughout the New Testament. Expressing God's heart to others is the evidence, fulfillment, and purpose of the new life in the believer.

As you carefully read the following passages consider what it means to display God's image. I made some brief comments to emphasize this connection between righteousness and loving others well.

Ephesians 5:1–2
Therefore, be imitators of God as dear children. And walk in love, as Christ also has loved us and given Himself for us, an offering and a sacrifice to God for a sweet- smelling aroma.

Note how Paul encourages us to love in the way Jesus did. Just as Christ's sacrifice replaced the Old Testament requirements of sacrifice for atonement and pleased God, so our loving of others fulfills this place of pleasing God.

1 John 2:8–11
Again, a new commandment I write to you, which thing is true in Him and in you, because the darkness is passing away, and the true light is already shining. He who says he is in the

light, and hates his brother, is in darkness until now. He who loves his brother abides in the light, and there is no cause for stumbling in him. But he who hates his brother is in darkness and walks in darkness, and does not know where he is going, because the darkness has blinded his eyes.

John expresses how the believers' behavior toward others is the litmus test for salvation. If there is a contradiction in ones love toward God and his or her love toward others, John boldly asserts that such a person walks in darkness.

Matthew 5:44
But I say to you, love your enemies, bless those who curse you, do good to those who hate you, and pray for those who spitefully use you and persecute you, that you may be sons of your Father in heaven; for He makes His sun rise on the evil and on the good, and sends rain on the just and on the unjust.

Your identity as a child of God is evident in the way you love those who are intent on being your adversary.

Colossians 3:12–17
Therefore, as the elect of God, holy and beloved, put on tender mercies, kindness, humility, meekness, longsuffering; bearing with one another, and forgiving one another, if anyone has a complaint against another; even as Christ forgave you, so you also must do. But above all these things put on love, which is the bond of perfection. And let the peace of God rule in your hearts, to which also you were called in one body; and be thankful. Let the word of Christ dwell in you

richly in all wisdom, teaching and admonishing one another in psalms and hymns and spiritual songs, singing with grace in your hearts to the Lord. And whatever you do in word or deed, do all in the name of the Lord Jesus, giving thanks to God the Father through Him.

This practice of loving people well is the new life into which we are saved. Paul shows us how to merge the reality of our new nature into our thoughts. He says, "Let the word of Christ dwell in you..." (Colossians 3:16). As we actively listen to and obey the voice of Jesus in our conscience, we will find ourselves identifying with His nature.

1 Thessalonians 4:9
But concerning brotherly love you have no need that I should write to you, for you yourselves are taught by God to love one another.

1 Timothy 1:5
Now, the purpose of the commandment is love from a pure heart, from a good conscience, and from sincere faith.

Hebrews 13:1
Let brotherly love continue. Do not forget to entertain strangers, for by so doing some have unwittingly entertained angels.

1 Peter 1:22
Since you have purified your souls in obeying the truth through the Spirit in sincere love of the brethren, love one another fervently with a pure heart, having been born again, not of corruptible seed but incorruptible, through the word

of God which lives and abides forever.

1 Peter 4:8–10
And above all things, have fervent love for one another. For 'love will cover a multitude of sins.' Be hospitable to one another without grumbling. As each one has received a gift, minister it to one another, as good stewards of the manifold grace of God.

1 John 3:10
In this the children of God and the children of the devil are manifest: Whoever does not practice righteousness is not of God, nor is he who does not love his brother.

1 John 3:23
And this is His commandment: that we should believe on the name of His Son Jesus Christ and love one another, as He gave us commandment.

1 John 4:7–8
Beloved, let us love one another, for love is of God; and everyone who loves is born of God and knows God. He who does not love does not know God, for God is love.

1 John 4:10–11
In this is love, not that we loved God, but that He loved us and sent His Son to be the propitiation for our sins. Beloved, if God so loved us, we also ought to love one another.

1 John 4:21
And this commandment we have from Him: that he who

loves God must love his brother also.

2 John 5
And now I plead with you, lady, not as though I wrote a new commandment to you, but that which we have had from the beginning: that we love one another.

In each of these passages, we see how loving behavior expresses the righteous nature we have. How we love is a direct extension of God's righteous nature through us.

The Evidence

In Galatians 5:22, Paul indicates how we can know the Holy Spirit is in a person. He writes, "The fruit of the Spirit is love, joy, peace, longsuffering, kindness, goodness, faithfulness, gentleness, self-control." Here the word "fruit" implies actions that result from a default way of thinking. We can know the Holy Spirit resides in a person when we see these unique qualities naturally, or should we say supernaturally, evident.

Often this passage is presented as motivation to muster up nine different qualities, or "fruits" of the Spirit. However, the text indicates the word "fruit" is singular, meaning the attributes of love, joy, peace, longsuffering, and such are mutually present. If this evidence of the Spirit is how we should behave, it has to be a work of the Spirit and not merely an isolated determination of our will.

We can say to ourselves; I have the Holy Spirit and He has self-control; therefore, I have self-control. He is loving, so I can love. He is joyful, so I can have joy in my situation. With statements like this we can lean into the ability God has placed in us.

We can rightly believe the Holy Spirit's presence is evidenced by one's ability to practice a spiritual gift. However, in light of the numerous passages listed above, this may not be completely accurate. Yes, we should desire and even pursue spiritual gifts. But if we don't pursue loving people, our desire is distorted.

In 1 Corinthians 14:1, Paul shows us how to prioritize spiritual gifts with love. He writes, "Pursue love, and desire spiritual gifts" (1 Cor. 14:1). We are to make loving others the first priority in our growth. This thought is plainly reflected in 1 Corinthians 13:1–3, the beginning of the well-known, "love chapter."

When our motivation to serve God is manifest in our love for people, we enter into the realm of life which Paul terms as "walking in the Spirit" (Galatians 5:16–18). This practice moves us from seeking our own fulfillment to loving others well. This is the one law we are given to fulfill.

The Life You Want

In our day to day over-marketed culture, we at times default to the question of, "what is in this for me?" What benefit is there in freely giving of your time, energy and righteous identity within? In fulfilling this one commandment of loving others as God loves, there's a promise which is often overlooked. Jesus tells us of it in John 15:9–12. He says,

As the Father loved Me, I also have loved you; abide in My love. If you keep My commandments, you will abide in My love, just as I have kept My Father's commandments and abide in His love. These things I have spoken to you, that My joy may remain in you, and that your joy may be full. This is

My commandment, that you love one another as I have loved you.

Jesus shows us how our obedience to His command to love others will fuel in us in a perpetual joy of experiencing His love. How much of God's love can we experience in this place of giving of ourselves? Jesus promises we can have the same joy He has (John 15:8-14). We will experience the same delight and feel the same fullness of joy when we love others in the way Jesus did.

Now, let's be clear, this joy Jesus experienced was born in a love for His Father that translated into a love for us. In the same way we are invited to express our love for the Father through the practice of loving others. In this, Jesus promises, we will find fulfillment. This self-sacrificing joy is not without the challenges of pain, but the end result is the fulfillment of being able to love like God loves.

What was the joy Jesus aimed to capture? In Hebrews 12:2, we see it was in the giving of His life. The writer states how Jesus, "... for the joy that was set before Him endured the cross, despising the shame, and has sat down at the right hand of the throne of God" (Hebrews 12:2).

I know this may not sound so enticing at first, but moving into the place of laying down our life to be the expression of God to others is the calling God places on each of His children. It is a joy you can only find and appreciate after the willing sacrifice of loving like Jesus does. This is the righteous nature through which we can reveal God to a broken world.

Though the realization of the righteous identity within us is the first step, there still remains a process through which we grow into the identity we possess. This journey of living out the righteous identity doesn't always come easily. The battle begins in our mind. As we believe we are righteous, the Holy Spirit works in our belief system to disarm every lie which tells us we are not.

Chapter 9
The War Within

"Whether a man lives or dies in vain can be measured only by the way he faces his own problems, by the success or failure of the inner conflict within his own soul. And of this no one may know save God."

-James Bryant Conant

"God, I'll never do it again," Thomas said under his breath. He had mumbled his promise a hundred times before, but this time he wanted it to stick. It began, as it usually did, with a scandalous preview on Netflix. The R-rating removed all doubt as to what kind of movie this was. It was a sexually explicit movie, but as Thomas settled on his couch with a bag of chips, he justified his desire to watch it, saying to himself, "Well, it has some historical basis." His thoughts, as many times before, quickly spiraled down a slope of excuses until he silenced the feeling of conviction in his gut.

Midway through the film, he ashamedly turned off the screen, and the voices began. "What are you doing? You're not a Christian. You're a just another pervert trapped in a porn problem. If you really were a Christian, then you wouldn't do this. What if someone knows? What if your church friends know? What will happen if someone finds out?" Fear seized his mind. "If God cared about me,

He'd help me," he said to himself. He was disgusted by his addiction, but nothing seemed to change. "I might as well just go on and watch whatever makes me happy," he resolved, "since no one cares, and I'm not hurting anyone."

In his teenage years, his body would physically tremble when the eerie, dark presence of lust came over him, but now he had grown almost comfortable with the feeling. He felt distant from God. "If there is a God," he would tell himself, "He'd help me get me out of this." Thomas felt alone and abandoned. He often prayed for an escape from his bondage, but nothing happened. "Is there a way out?" He would often ask himself. "When I get married, this lust thing will go away," he tried to convince himself, looking for hope.

His internal monologue of fear and desperation occurred frequently. As a follow-up, he'd resolve to pray and fast from food for a few days to stabilize his feelings of weakness. He'd commit to read the whole Bible within a few months' time and to do other seemingly spiritual tasks. A few days would go by, and he would feel as if God favored him again. But not long after a parade of good behavior, he'd be back in the miserable chains of pornography. The cycle would begin anew with more resolutions and more inevitable failure.

We sat in my office as he despondently asked, "How do I get out of this?" "There's not a quick solution," I said. "When did this begin?" He told me his addiction began out of innocent sexual curiosity. But when the harshness of an abusive father and a complicit mother left him feeling abandoned, he turned to pornography to escape.

During his descent into addiction, he committed to follow Jesus at a revival meeting at his church, and he was able to resist the temptation for a few months. After a few weeks had passed, the disappointment of not making any friends in the church, and a failed romantic hope, he was alone with his pain once again. In his moment of weakness, the all too familiar demons of perversion welcomed him back with open arms. He succumbed to the temptation again.

"How long have you been following Jesus?" I asked. "Ten years," he replied. For ten years, he had been victim to this cycle. Since that first meeting, we began a long journey of restoring Thomas back to His identity in Jesus. It began with him choosing to believe he was given the righteous identity of Jesus at the moment of his salvation.

Regardless of his feelings of shame, he had to keep telling himself, even in the face of failure, "I am the righteousness of God in Jesus" (2 Corinthians 5:21). The more he said it, the more he believed it, the more deliverance he experienced. With the regular intake of God's word in his life, Thomas not only believed he was free but now enjoys the freedom Christ gave to him. Does he battle the impulse to give in to lust? Yes. But his ability to resist has grown stronger as he daily chooses to walk in the Spirit.

No matter the addiction or weakness, we all are susceptible to the cycle of sin. It occurs when a shameful act of sin is followed by confession and then by resolving or promising to be better. Finally, in condemnation, usually after a glorious period of success, we fail. This cycle continues because of a mistaken belief.

This is the cycle or "law of sin" from which Paul says we are free. He writes in Romans 8:2-4, "For the law of the Spirit of life in Christ Jesus has made me free from the law of sin and death. For what the law could not do in that it was weak through the flesh, God did by sending His own Son in the likeness of sinful flesh, on account of sin: He condemned sin in the flesh, that the righteous requirement of the law might be fulfilled in us who do not walk according to the flesh but according to the Spirit."

The law of sin and death is a truth we all understand, even if we haven't defined it in our thinking. We sin and then we invoke a moral rule or standard upon ourselves to feel righteous again. But, because we lack the power to be righteous, we fail again and again. The condemnation of our sinful nature weighs on us. It will eventually crush the hope we have of being righteous. On the other hand, the law of the spirit of life says, "We are righteous." We are righteous because Jesus is righteous, and he gave us His righteous identity.

Our faith in Him, which is reflected in our relationship with Him, empowers us to believe we are righteous, as He is. We are not righteous because the temptation of sin is gone. We are not righteous because we merely ask for God's forgiveness. We are righteous because the presence of Jesus is in us and the desire for sin is diminished because we find our fulfillment in Him.

More Than Confessions

Like Thomas, we've all prayed the "God, I'm sorry," prayer. However, this admission cannot bring us into the righteous nature we desire. Though the confession of sin is a healthy practice in relationships with others (James 5:16), we often elevate the act of confession to be equal to the saving ability of the Holy Spirit. Confession is only transformational when it is practiced with the correct belief.

Let me explain. When Jesus made atonement for all sins, he didn't merely atone for the sins you would confess. The application of His atonement was for every human for all time. John the Baptist introduced Jesus to the world saying, "Behold the lamb of God who takes away the sins of the world" (John 1:29, 1 John 2:2). Christ atoned for all sins. Therefore, sin is not the reason sinners are separated from God. The cause of eternal separation is when people choose not to believe in Jesus as God's son (John 1:12, John 3:15-16, John 3:36, John 6:47, Mark 16:16, Romans 1:17).

The confession of sin and the acceptance of Christ's salvation are not the same. In 1 John 1:9 we read, "If we confess our sins, he is faithful and just to forgive us and cleanse us from all unrighteousness." The word confess here (homo-logo-men) holds a unique idea which has significant depth.[38] Dissecting the Greek word, "homo-logo-men" to the three core ideas which compose it, aids us in understanding the meaning of confession.

The first part is "homo," which means to consist of the same thing. For example, "homo" in the word homonym means two words that have the same sound. The second part, "logo" means a spoken word. Finally, the suffix "men" refers to the one who speaks. If we put these three root words together, confess means "to say the same thing." Therefore John 1:9 can be understood to say, "if we confess (say the same thing about) our sins, He (Jesus) is faithful and just to forgive us and cleanse us from unrighteousness (or the lack of our right-nature)."

When we agree with God's view of our unrighteous behavior, this admission is a recognition that we are acting outside of the identity we have been given. When we do this, Jesus promises to cleanse us of the unrighteousness or non-God-like nature within us. When we come into agreement with Jesus' view of sin, he has promised to

---

38 Michel, O. (1964–). ὁμολογέω, ἐξομολογέω, ἀνθομολογέομαι, ὁμολογία, ὁμολογουμένως. G. Kittel, G. W. Bromiley, & G. Friedrich (Eds.), Theological dictionary of the New Testament (electronic ed., Vol. 5, p. 201). Grand Rapids, MI: Eerdmans.

remove barriers to belief from our thinking. Barriers to believing in the right nature we possess will result in lies which shape our behavior. Our old nature can only be empowered in one way: it is fueled by a lie. Believing a lie will cause you to behave in contradiction to your righteous identity.

The greatest lie we believe is that we are not righteous. It is the lie the enemy perpetuates in our thinking. He compares our behavior to our belief and dismisses the nature of God deposited into our spirit. Once we refute the lie, then the belief or faith that we possess the right nature of God will direct our spirit to behave in a way that is out of love for the Father. How do we deal with our past unrighteous behavior? We need only to accept again God's decision for our sins. He says we are forgiven, and we need to have faith in that promise. We were forgiven in the moment of Christ's atonement. Confession in this context is an expression of our belief in Jesus' sacrifice, which was accomplished centuries ago.

Coming back to the earlier story of Thomas, he didn't experience freedom until he began to say the same thing that God said about himself and his addiction. The Holy Spirit unfolded to Thomas the freedom God already had for him. He told Thomas that he had the right-nature of God in Christ Jesus (2 Corinthians 5:21). The more Thomas believed, the more freedom he experienced. Freedom came when he perceived himself as God did. In this, Thomas removed many lies he had thought about himself and God.

When faced with temptation, he began a dialogue with the Holy Spirit. He would say to himself, "I am the righteousness (right-nature) of God in Jesus." With this belief and the correct use of confession, Thomas began to draw out of himself the right-nature, which had been dormant in him. This is Paul's emphatic point in Romans 10:10. He says, "For with the heart one believes unto righteousness, and with the mouth, confession is made unto salvation." With our heart, we believe in the right-nature God has placed in us, and the result is our mouth declaring the salvation we possess. This is how victory against the enemy of unbelief is won.

Maintaining the Righteous Identity

You may not always be fighting the devil when you feel trapped in temptation. Rather, you may be contending with your own broken system of believing. False beliefs cripple our faith and empower the enemy to manifest his will in our lives. When you exercise your faith in self-condemnation, believing you are not righteous, then your behavior will follow. When you believe you are bound in sin, you are bound to sin by faith. When you believe you have been freed, you can experience freedom. Your believing, whether it is in God's word or your fears, will produce a result.

How do you keep yourself free of the lies which seek to capture you? By firmly establishing the truth of God's word in your mind and heart. Truth must first enter your mind before it can become a weapon for your spirit to use. Often, we hear the Christian jargon which compels us to "get God's Word in your heart." What does this mean?

It means we need to consciously place God's word into our thinking by consistently reading His words, praying and memorizing scripture. How is this done? By daily opening up conversation with Jesus as you read and apply the Scriptures. In this process, not only will you strengthen your relationship with God, but revelation will make an impact in your behavior. How then could you lose the freedom you have been given by Jesus?

Believers who have been infused with the righteous nature of Jesus can only be derailed in one way: when they repeatedly choose to believe a lie. What is the lie that often cripples faith? The lie is that you still have a sinful nature after you have received salvation. Compounding this deception, Christians often suggest you need to reach a certain benchmark of maturity to be confident in the righteousness you desire. Of course, the voice of the enemy needs only to nudge our self-doubts to form a convincing lie. If we do not know how to recognize and resist the enemy's voice, we can find ourselves abandoning the identity we have in God for one that is contrary to our divine nature (2 Peter 1:4).

We know the nature of God is in us when we feel the collision between a desire to be righteous and the deception that we are not. When we allow sinful thoughts to enter our thinking, a battle erupts in us. In this war within us, the voice of the Holy Spirit also enters to tell us who we are in Jesus. Peter warns us to "...abstain from fleshly lusts which war against the soul..." (1 Peter 2:11). The conflict of the universe is not commencing in a distant spiritual dimension. No, it is happening right now in the few inches that span between your ears.

In the mind of every follower of Jesus, a war is being waged against the resident Spirit of God. As a result, a disciple is dominated by the voice he or she chooses to obey. Paul clarifies this by asking, "Do you not know that to whom you present yourselves slaves to obey, you are that one's slaves whom you obey, whether of sin leading to death, or of obedience leading to righteousness?" (Romans 6:16).

The spirit realm does exist, and the power of the enemy does destroy millions who are complicit to his work. However, the battle first begins in your thoughts. Only from a place of confidence in our righteous nature can we exercise the authority we have into the realm of the spirit.

With God's opinion about you planted deep in your heart, the Holy Spirit can use your faith to bring out His righteous nature in you. This key strategy of knowing the right nature you have begins by knowing what God says about you. We see this dynamic of combating the lies of the enemy demonstrated in Jesus' battle against temptation (Matthew 4:1-11, Luke 3:21-22). The devil enticed Jesus to prove His identity.

Let me explain why this was a temptation. When the devil posed the question to Jesus, "If you are the Son of God...," he wasn't asking for a DNA test. The question is presented in what Greek scholars call *the first-class condition*. This means the question is assumed to be true, at least from the point of view of the author; therefore, it should be translated "since" (instead of "if") for English readers. The devil is not doubting Jesus' divinity but was tempting Him to misuse or abuse His powers.[39]

This same temptation comes to every disciple of Jesus. "If you are righteous," the enemy will say to you, "then you would_____." Fill in the blank with all the good behaviors you feel like you should be doing. His condemning voice says to us, "You should be a better parent, spouse, employee, etc...." You may have been pressured to prove your righteousness with outward behaviors like methodical Bible reading, excessive prayer, financial contributions, or other spiritualized behaviors.

Though these disciplines are healthy, they are the outworking of righteousness within you, not the proof of it. If you do them as means

---

39 Utley, R. J. (2000). *The First Christian Primer: Matthew* (Vol. Volume 9, p. 27). Marshall, TX: Bible Lessons International.

to convince yourself of the righteous identity you already have, then you will fall into the temptation which Jesus faced. It would not have been a sin for Jesus to miraculously make bread. In fact, we read of Him miraculously making bread at other times, but to do so to prove His identity to the enemy would submission to the enemy's condemning voice. By not miraculously creating bread in his moment of temptation, Jesus was able to escape condemnation How did he do this?

Only a few weeks before his temptation, Jesus approached his cousin, John, to be baptized. As Jesus rose out of the waters of the Jordan, God affirmed His identity. Luke records the moment saying, "Jesus also being baptized, and praying, the heaven was opened, and the Holy Ghost descended in a bodily shape like a dove upon him, and a voice came from heaven, which said, Thou art my beloved Son; in thee I am well pleased" (Luke 3:21–22).

One would think, Jesus could have easily cited his recent baptism experience to the devil as proof of His sonship, but Jesus didn't utilize his personal experience to affirm his identity. He pulled upon a greater source. He directed the enemy to the Scriptures He knew. Jesus modeled for us how to resist the condemning voice of the enemy. Just as Jesus spoke and behaved in the identity of the Scriptures He believed and professed, you can do the same.

As you fight the lies of the enemy by believing what God has said about you, you'll find your deep faith in and repetition of God's word in your thoughts will establish your faith and repel the lies of the enemy. How can you make God's Word become your default response? Simple and consistent repetition of reading and believing what God has said.

From Head to Heart

I remember learning this principle of establishing the truth of scripture in my own heart. As a second grader, my family lived in a house that had a breezeway between our back-patio door and a tool room. On various nights it fell to me to walk through this area to take our garbage bags to the larger trashcans in our yard. There was enough moonlight to contort the shapes of trees and poles into hideous goblins. With a healthy imagination, such as mine, one would almost faint at the sights I saw. The trash delivery, however, had to be done.

Around this time, at school I was handed the weekly scripture to memorize. The large pink and red card read, "For God has not given us a spirit of fear, but of power and of love and of a sound mind" (2 Timothy 1:7). To my fourth-grade mind, it was just another assignment. But something unusual happened a few days after memorizing that card. It was my job to once again journey through the dark alley of my fear and imagination.

As I fearfully stepped out of my house that little scripture came to mind. I said it to myself silently the first time, then with a little adrenaline flowing I recited it aloud in hope for some confidence. By the time I had repeated it a dozen times, I was shouting it into the darkness and boldly marching my way across the twenty-foot stretch. I'm sure it would have been comical to watch a little Indian child shouting out scriptures under the moonlight while bearing bags of trash on his shoulders, but it imprinted the power of God's word in my little soul.

Something was happening inside of me. Without realizing it, I was aligning my thinking with the reality of who I was in Jesus. Was

I afraid? Yes, but something different happened that night. I felt my strength against the fear grow. Ever since then, that scripture has transformed from a memory assignment to core belief.

What we repeat to ourselves again and again will evolve into a deep-seated belief. You may say, "Aren't you just brainwashing yourself?" Yes! And truth be told, everyone is brainwashed into the core beliefs they hold. Brainwashing is inevitable, but you might find it beneficial to choose exactly how you are brainwashed. Reading, repeating, and meditating on the scriptures will embolden the righteousness Jesus has placed into your spirit.

During my early years of ministry as a youth pastor, I found myself utilizing this same method of realizing my identity in Jesus. I had become too busy to dedicate time to meditating on God's word. I felt my spiritual life slipping even though I was serving as a youth pastor. I prayed for a solution to get my mind back into the right nature God had deposited in me.

I eventually found myself in a small Christian bookstore purchasing a New Testament audio cassette series, read by Alexander Scourby. This happened in a time long before cell phones, iPods, or digital media. I spent an hour a day in my $900, beat-up Ford Escort Coupe, during my commutes to school and church, listening to God's word. I listened to the book of Ephesians over, and over again. I went to sleep with it playing and went about my morning routine with Mr. Scourby reading in my ear. I found my heart firmly established in the revelation of who I was in Jesus. To this day, this practice is a powerful tool I use.

Through numerous platforms and apps, there's no reason you

cannot have the Word of God implanted into your mind regularly. The repetition of hearing God's word will plant the seeds of your identity deep in your heart. It really is this simple and powerful. From hearing, you can move to believing what God says, and rejecting the lies that keep you from living in your identity: one who has the right-nature of God.

The Right Way to Read

How you capture and affirm the righteous identity you have is highlighted in Paul's comment to the Galatians when he says,

> For he who sows to (cultivates) his flesh will of the flesh reap corruption, but he who sows to (cultivates) the Spirit will of the Spirit reap everlasting life. And let us not grow weary while doing good, for in due season we shall reap if we do not lose heart. (Galatians 6:8-9)

The more you feed yourself God's truth, the greater freedom you will experience in your relationship with Jesus and with others. If you believe the lies which feed doubts about your righteous nature before God, you will find yourself starved of the life you were created to experience. Your eternal salvation may not be jeopardized, but will you miss out on a fulfilled life.

God has made you to be a part of   His redeeming plan in the world, freeing others to be with Him. There are many things which come to distract you from the calling you have, but you have a choice each day to enter God's realm of truth or to live dormant in your deceptions.

Let me close this chapter with a word of advice Paul gave to Timothy, his young disciple from the city of Lystra. He warns Timothy to readily view his identity as one who is approved before God. Timothy struggled with doubt of his validity to serve in Ephesus. His doubts may have been fueled by his young age or his non-Jewish background, but Paul didn't entertain his doubts. He was charged to, "Be diligent to present yourself approved to God, a worker who does not need to be ashamed, rightly dividing the word of truth" (2 Timothy 2:15).

In this statement, Paul indicates how the very scriptures can be become a tool of condemnation if they are not understood correctly. They must be read through the lens of one's approval before God.

When scriptures are used to stir feelings of guilt, shame, and fear of judgement, they are not being used correctly. As you read the scriptures, they should bring you to a realization of the righteous identity God has placed in you. Only by the intentional meditation of God's word in our thoughts can you break free from the systemic patterns of self-condemnation. *You can never reach the fullness of your identity in Jesus until you believe you are as righteous as He says you are.*

For Thomas, the process of firmly believing he was righteous took time. It took months of binging on scriptures, teachings, and Sunday sermons, concerning his identity in Jesus. However, months later, he broke free from the chains of the shame and addiction which once gripped his soul. To this day he is a free man fully walking in the identity which Jesus provided for him.

Chapter 10
God in You - Forgiving

"We must develop and maintain the capacity to forgive. He who is devoid of the power to forgive is devoid of the power to love. There is some good in the worst of us and some evil in the best of us. When we discover this, we are less prone to hate our enemies."
-Martin Luther King, Jr.

We sat quietly on the brown, padded seats of a Waffle House booth. John, a friend from years' past, requested a meeting a few days prior. We hadn't talked since our college days, and even then, our discussions were not of a serious nature. Lines of distress furrowed his brow as he began his story. "I hate my dad," he said. "Every time I see him, he manages to tick me off." John went on to reveal how his father verbally and physically abused him and his siblings for years. It was a well-kept family secret. A secret John was tired of carrying. The need for his dad's approval pushed him to do many things he now regretted.

On the outside John was a stellar young man. He was the captain of his high school football team, an honor graduate, and a leader among his classmates. On the inside, however, he was imprisoned. He never felt good enough for his dad's approval. Somehow this need spilled over into a need for approval from his wife, his boss, and other significant relationships. As we spoke, he realized he also felt he didn't have God's approval. Many of his days were filled with oppression and loneliness. He was a Christian by all indications, but he never felt like he experienced salvation in the same way everyone around him had. His wounds were inflicted deeply by a dad who was a celebrated church leader.

For years, John bore the rage-filled beatings of his dad on Saturday evenings and then watched the parade of a spiritual dad on Sunday mornings. Now, forty or so years later, John struggled with discerning the character of God apart from the behavior of his dad. When misfortune happened to him, he felt God was angry. The war in his mind was one of constant repentance for sins he may or may not have committed. He felt he always had to appease an unpredictable, mood-shifting God.

Tears streamed down his face as he told me of how he could not bear the weight of his childhood secrets anymore. "How do I get these feelings out?" He asked. "I've forgiven my dad, but he keeps jacking me up every time I see him."

John's emotional trauma is far too common. Many of us have relationships in our lives that are hurtful, and we don't have the luxury of walking away from them. To band-aid relationships like these with the "forgive and forget," catchphrase isn't good enough. True forgiveness, however, can release you from the pain of past memories and harmful relationships.

You can only experience the full power of forgiveness when you must forgive out of the righteous identity within you. It is no coincidence how the exercise of forgiving is commonly the first test of the righteous identity in us.

When Jesus rose from the grave and appeared to His disciples the first test of their new righteousness dealt with their ability to forgive. He breathed on them and said, "Receive the Holy Spirit." (John 20:19). Then He said, "If you forgive the sins of any, they are forgiven them; if you retain the sins of any, they are retained." Who did they need to forgive?

If we take Jesus' statement in context, Jesus was empowering them to forgive those who had him murdered him a few days prior. How could the disciples be the proclaimers of Jesus' resurrection if they harbored unforgiveness toward the masses of those who had chanted "crucify Him." They needed a power greater than what they possessed to forgive.

Jesus pulled the disciples into their new forgiving identity as He breathed His own Spirit into them. As we consider the directive which Jesus gave to his disciples, and by virtue every believer, we must note first how He gave us the power to forgive just as He forgives. On one hand this is amazing, but you can only appreciate it as you discover the fullness of God's forgiving nature.

In the concluding thought of his Galatian letter, Paul brings his readers to the practical application of God's right nature in us. He identifies how we exercise God's forgiving and restoring identity when he writes, "Brethren, if a man is overtaken in any trespass, you who are spiritual restore such a one in a spirit of gentleness, considering yourself lest you also be tempted. Bear one another's burdens, and so fulfill the law of Christ."[40] How does this kind of forgiving and restoring happen?

40 The New King James Version. (1982). (Ga 6:1–2). Nashville: Thomas Nelson.

Forgiving is God's Idea

First, we must take a step back to realize forgiveness is an extension of God's identity. By this I mean God doesn't have a quality of forgiving, rather He embodies the meaning of forgiveness. As God is in us, we can discover His identity working through us to forgive those who have harmed us. Paul clearly makes this point in his letter to the Corinthians when he says,

> "...God, who has reconciled us to Himself through Jesus Christ, and has given us the ministry of reconciliation, that is, that God was in Christ reconciling the world to Himself, not imputing their trespasses to them, and has committed to us the word of reconciliation."[41]

To forgive someone who has deeply hurt you takes more than pious determination. It takes God-infused ability to gracefully let go of an offense. Forgiving someone who may or may not care about you takes a measure of emotional vulnerability. It means humbling your heart and admitting the pain you feel and your need for healing.

In the context of close relationships, this is difficult. To exercise forgiveness well, you must trust this first step of bringing your heart to a realization of what you've experienced and then ask the Holy Spirit to empower you and to pull your righteous identity forward in your thoughts. You are a child of God and, by virtue of God's nature in you, your heart longs for the healing balm of forgiveness. God's nature of compassion toward those who willfully hurt Him is in you. As you forgive, God's loving nature is revealed to those who are blind to His compassion.

Every religion and numerous factions within Christianity por-

---

41 The New King James Version. (1982). (2 Co 5:18–19). Nashville: Thomas Nelson.

tray God to be one who is vindictive and emotionally distant. This couldn't be further from the truth. King David, the man whom God identified as a pursuer of His heart, tells us,

> The Lord is gracious and full of compassion, slow to anger and great in mercy. The Lord is good to all, and His tender mercies are over all His works. [42]

By default, God is loving and forgiving. The disciple John, Jesus' closest follower, records God's essence to be one of pure love. In 1 John 4:7-11 he writes,

> Beloved, let us love one another, for love is of God; and everyone who loves is born of God and knows God. He who does not love does not know God, for God is love. In this the love of God was manifested toward us, that God has sent His only begotten Son into the world, that we might live through Him. In this is love, not that we loved God, but that He loved us and sent His Son to be the propitiation for our sins. Beloved, if God so loved us, we also ought to love one another.

God's nature is love and when He infuses His nature into the believer, they are commissioned to be carriers of His love. God's love is demonstrated, according to this text, in forgiving sin. Forgiving is a part of your righteous identity.

Forgiveness is fundamental to the righteous identity you have in you. It fuels every healthy relationship and friendship. Why is this important to note? Aside from the obvious reasons, relationships are the conduit through which God speaks to us. Relationships are also the means through which God revels Himself the world. So many

---

42 The New King James Version. (1982). (Ps 145:8–9). Nashville: Thomas Nelson.

have come to conclude that God is angry with humanity. I have found the number one reason people turn from Jesus is because they mistake him to be like the last unforgiving Christian they experienced.

Few reject a church community because they read an offensive passage in the Bible. What usually drives people from the church are those who portray God to be critical and condemning. Yes, *truths about God are learned in the scriptures, but the understanding of what God is like is often experienced through relationships* with those who claim to know Him.

When godly people become bitter, unforgiving, or even behave harshly toward each other, everyone is alarmed because this behavior doesn't reflect the righteous nature. When Jesus brought the truth of salvation to the world, he didn't deliver it to us a book. He inscribed it in the relationships He held with those He loved. The disciples were not merely pious students. They became the message through whom God desired to communicate. Jesus embodied the full message of God's nature and desire for us (John 1:14). In like fashion, Christ's disciples must be the message He desires to proclaim to a lost world.

What is the message God wants to relay through us? He is forgiving. He paid a costly price to forgive us. He forgave us when we didn't deserve it. He didn't wait until we were repentant to forgive us. If we believe in this forgiveness, then we have no room to respond in bitterness toward those who offend us. When we freely give the forgiveness we have received, it will open the door to transformation within our own heart and mind (Mark 10:8, Matthew 6:15).

Forgiving is Perpetual

Secondly, forgiving is a repeated behavior. This means when you forgive someone, it extends beyond a single moment of decision. You must choose again and again to not view those who have hurt you as worthy of judgement. If you've said, "I forgave, but God will judge them," then you've not forgiven. Hoping God will judge someone's wrongdoing on your behalf is asking God to be an accomplice to your bitterness. So how can you begin the process of forgiving? It starts with simple prayers toward those who have harmed you. Every time the thought of a past offense or offender comes to mind, you can pray, "Jesus, I forgive _____ for (what they did)."

At first, you may have to pray this a few dozen times a day. It is hard, but as you push through the impulse to meditate on your pain, it gets easier. You may need to dialogue with Jesus until you reach a decision to forgive. I've gone through the practice of saying,

> *"Jesus, when (person's name) did this... (describe what happed to you) it made me feel (describe how you feel, and be honest.), but I am choosing to forgive them. I forgive because You have forgiven me. Remove bitterness from me. Let me see them as you see them."*

It starts with a simple prayer, but you can allow the healing to begin in your heart which will mature you into the full nature of who you are in Jesus.

We all have heard the phrase "forgive and forget." However, this isn't realistic. In the forgiving of someone, you will have the reoccurring memory of the wrong done to you. Each time you remember, however, you can displace the pain by declaring your forgiveness toward your offender. Each time you say, "I have forgiven_____," you will find strength to forgive again and again.

In time, the emotional attachment you had toward an incident or against someone will be drained of its power to torment you. This is how the love of God working through you can remove bitterness. On another note, When the love of God is at work through you, it doesn't eliminate the need for boundaries with someone who is an abuser, it simply means you can see someone as God does and push through the negative feelings you have and forgive them.

Now let's consider the forgetting part of forgiving. Many believe that God forgives and forget our sins. To this belief I'd ask, "How does an all-knowing God not know the things you have done?" He knows and will always know, but he chooses to forgive. God knows your sin long before you commit it. Before we could sin against Him, He knew our broken nature and intended for an atonement to be provided. God planned to forgive you long before the world was created. This is why we read in Revelation 3:8 how Jesus is "the Lamb slain from the foundation of the world." [43]

We can understand this kind of forgiveness in the context of relationship. The ones we love most, we readily forgive. With this predisposition to forgive, our nature is set to love without giving opportunity for offense. Most parents can identify this disposition to forgive. We know our kids are going to mess up. They are going to make painful mistakes. Some of those mistakes we will never forget. However, because of our love for our kids, and our identity which we see in them, we naturally draw them close to us in their time of error and call their identity up to who we believe them to be.

43 The New King James Version. (1982). (Ps 145:8–9). Nashville: Thomas Nelson.

It is almost natural to look beyond a child's immaturity and mistakes so you can love them in spite of their selfishness. Is God any less of a parent? No. He is counting on His love for us to mature us into His forgiving nature. God's love is perpetually shown to us in His forgiving nature. He has always and will always bear the consequence of our broken nature in forgiving us. How often does God forgive us? Whether we ask for it or not, He forgives us every morning. Every morning God's mercy is renewed to us (Lamentations 3:22). Even though He knows in great detail everything we've done, He chooses to not recall our sins because of His love for us.

Why does God do this? In Proverbs 17:9 we read, "He who covers a transgression seeks love…" God is seeking a relationship with us, so He covers our sin. In Hebrews 8:12, God speaks of how he will remove the guilt of sin from us in saying, "I will be merciful to their unrighteousness, and their sins and their lawless deeds I will remember no more."[44] The word *remember* in this text means, "to recall information from memory, but without necessarily the implication that persons have actually forgotten."[45] God perpetually chooses not to bring back into his remembrance the sins of the people He loves.

Just as God models forgiveness to you, so you can duplicate His right-nature in your relationships. Few, if any, have the ability to actually forget negative experiences, however, you can refuse to process the negative thoughts associated with an injustice in your mind. You can do this by replacing this with a willingness to say, "I have forgiven." This is how perpetual forgiveness is applied.

To forgive wholly you must rely on God's power in you to forgive. Although you draw on God's nature in you to do it, it still remains as a decision you must make. God Himself cannot make you forgive.

44 The New King James Version. (1982). (Heb 8:12). Nashville: Thomas Nelson.
45 Louw, J. P., & Nida, E. A. (1996). Greek-English lexicon of the New Testament: based on semantic domains (electronic ed. of the 2nd edition., Vol. 1, p. 346). New York: United Bible Societies.

You must forgive. When you forgive, your action may not always be affirmed by how you feel. You may rarely feel like forgiving. If we wait until we feel like it, that moment may never come. Because forgiving is a choice, you must courageously move through your feelings and forgive the ones who have hurt you. Then there is the hard part of dealing with the consequence of another's sin against you.

Forgiving Will Cost You More Than the Receiver.

Forgiveness is resolving to live with the consequences of someone's wrongdoing. This is hard to do, but once you make this decision, it will free you from repeatedly blaming the one who has hurt you. You have to take ownership of your situation, forgive, and believe God for His ability to carry on with the consequences of the wrong done to you. Forgiveness will always cost the one who forgives more than the one who receives. This is important to note because forgiving someone always has a cost.

The one who forgives will always pay a price that seems unfair. The cost to the forgiver is painful, but this is where the beauty of God's love enters. We don't forgive those who've hurt us because they deserve it. When someone needs to be forgiven, they often don't recognize their need for it. You will become unloving or cynical if you wait for people to realize their wrong and need for forgiveness. As you forgive, there is a greater chance your offenders will see the love God has for them.

Finally, here's the good news about forgiving. The forgiver always receives more joy than the receiver. It's true. When you forgive from your heart, it liberates you to love those who have intentionally hurt you. This even works when the ones who have hurt you don't feel they need to be forgiven. The cost of forgiving remains mostly unknown by most, but the joy He has in forgiving us is far greater than the joy we'll experience.

In Jesus' well-known parable of prodigal son, it is the Father who invokes the party, not the forgiven son. The Father calls for the best steaks to be served and the best clothes to be brought out for his son. How do you begin to enter the same joy God experiences in forgiving? It begins by taking the initial step of forgiving freely. As you do, you will find the righteous, God-like nature of forgiveness grow within you.

Dealing with Past Pain

As you grow in knowing the righteous identity you have, the roadblock of past hurt will come. Great books have been written to deal with weighty reality of pain and suffering. However, I want to offer a method which I've utilized in in dealing with past hurts. I've seen this response work in my life and in the lives of those with which I've counseled. When tragedy has happened in our lives, it's only natural to ask, "Why did God allow this to happen?" A difficulty in this question is the the assumption that God's response will bring a satisfactory response to our hearts; however, many times it will not.

God's reason for allowing suffering to touch our lives many times cannot be understood in the moment of pain. Even if we could understand the why, it in no way will alleviate the pain we feel. The loss of a loved one, a career, or personal possessions will not be soothed when God gives us an eternal response. I write this knowing many may object. You may say, "If God told me why, then I'd be able to cope." But the truth is that one "why" will only lead to another. Many times, our need for understanding can be traced back to a deeper lack of trust.

How then can you move forward in healing from painful past events? From the ancient story of Job, we find a hint. Job, after the loss of all his material possessions, his children, and his health found himself asking God "Why?" He had lived in his righteous identity to the best of his ability. However, in the story we see a greater narrative unfold. God was demonstrating to the devil and to future generations how His righteous nature could be infused into a man and how that man would not turn from Him in the midst of the most horrific adversity. God was proving His righteous identity in Job. He was demonstrating how His plan to redeem humanity would work.

Note God's perspective of Job before the tragedies occurred. He says to Satan, "Have you considered My servant Job, that there is none like him on the earth, a blameless and upright man, one who fears God and shuns evil?" (Job 1:8) God had a relationship with Job in which He trusted the identity of Job to be like His own— righteous. The devil argued with God that Job's devotion was a result of God's blessing on his life. God responded by allowing the enemy to remove all of Job's possessions and children. Job did not waiver.

He didn't understand what was happening, but He was resolute in his trust in God. Job responded to all his tragedy by saying, "Naked I came from my mother's womb, and naked shall I return there. The Lord gave, and the Lord has taken away; Blessed be the name of the Lord." The scriptures go on to say, "In all this Job did not sin nor charge God with wrong" (Job 1:21-22). Then the enemy returned to God to hear His absolute trust in Job. God says to him, "Have you considered My servant Job, that there is none like him on the earth, a blameless and upright man, one who fears God and shuns evil? And still he holds fast to his integrity, although you incited Me against him, to destroy him without cause" (Job 2:3). Job's righteous nature didn't fail under the loss.

The enemy takes another jab at God's righteous plan by saying, "all that a man has he will give for his life. But stretch out Your hand now, and touch his bone and his flesh, and he will surely curse You to Your face!" (Job 2:4-5). God gave the enemy permission to touch Job's health, and the story commences. The enemy "struck Job with painful boils from the sole of his foot to the crown of his head" (Job 2:7). How did Job respond? He said, "Shall we indeed accept good from God, and shall we not accept adversity?" The passage goes on to say, "In all this Job did not sin with his lips" (Job 2:10).

This resilience and trust in God is amazing and unnatural. Even when Job's wife pushed him saying, "Do you still hold fast to your integrity? Curse God and die!" Job held to his righteous nature. The story continues of his friends coming to him and urging him to question his righteousness. Was Job upset? Yes. Was he in great sorrow and pain? Yes. Did his circumstances change his identity in God? No. He patiently allowed the nature of God in him to lead him through the dark night of his soul.

Following the long parlay of questions between Job and his friends, God responds to Job. It is in this discussion, we see a pathway to healing. God asked Job, "Where were you when I laid the foundations of the earth? Tell Me, if you have understanding..." God asked Job the "where" question to emphasize a powerful truth. God was with Job in all his adversity, but Job was nonexistent when God was laying down the foundations of the natural and supernatural world.

The understanding Job wanted was limiterd by his finite ability to comprehend God's eternal existence. God, who existed long before the world's formation, extedned his companionshiop to Job in the darkness of his tragedies. God invited Job to realize how the stamina for enduring suffering could come from knowin His nearness to him. When we know God is with us, grief may not make sense, but God's closeness to us can alleviate and even heal our momentary sorrow. Job concluded his story by confessing, "I have heard of You by the hearing of the ear, but now my eye sees You." When Job saw God was with him, his healing began. I make this point to stress how healing can come into your heart. In the memories of past sorrows, healing can be applied as you ask God, "Show me where you were in my tragedy."

Let me reiterate this thought. Though you may not intend to blame God, or others, it is natural to ask why as a means of coping with the pain. When you ask why something happened, you will soon realize there's no answer that will bring healing. However, if you hear and see how God was with you in your moments of trauma, then His presence can bring healing to you.

Just as God asked Job the "where were you," question, you will find God's question to Job was the key to aiding him in dealing with his pain. God was there before Job and with him throughout the entire process of his pain. When you ask God to show you how He was with you in your pain, you will find He was closer to you in your brokenness than you were able to see (Psalm 34:18).

Where Was God?

Weeks after my initial meeting with John, we began to work through the specific memories of his father's abuse. He told me of times when he and his brother would endure beatings after which their backs would be red with welts and bruises. His mom would have to hide in their home for weeks to recover from a black eye. Once, while running from his dad, John fell into a wall-mounted heater and nearly cracked his skull. With blood streaming down his face, he only hoped his accidental suffering would appease his father's rage. Through his ten-year-old eyes I could see his horrors and my heart sank in anguish. "Why would God let this happen to me?" he asked as he concluded his story.

Closing his eyes, John sat in my office and painfully went back to the moments of abuse he could remember. In his mind he went back to his fourth-grade year. He was in deep water with his dad because of a bad report card and a culmination of poor choices. His dad was yelling at his mom and the argument ended in screams and sounds of violence.

Scared to death, John crawled into his bed, pulled the sheets over his head and prayed for help. He could hear his dad making his way through the house to his room. His bedroom door slammed open and the yelling began. After the cursing and degrading, John was commanded to stand by his bed. He quickly stood, quivering in fear. After a few more, "You're good for nothing," statements, John braced for the belt lashings. They hurt. They always hurt.

With tears streaming down his face, adult John remembered that night of beating with great clarity. He laid trembling in his bed after his father left his room. I asked John to look within his memory around his room and to ask Jesus, "Where were you?" As John did this, tears streamed down his face. "I can see him," He said. "He was seated right there by my bed. He's crying and saying, 'I am so sorry this happened to you.'"

Then John heard the assuring voice of Jesus reach through His memory. He said to him, "John, I was with you in all of those moments. I spoke often to your father, but he hardened his heart to my voice." The Lord went on to speak more to John and since that moment of hearing Jesus, the impact of those painful memories has been soothed. He encountered Jesus in his greatest time of need.

I would encourage you to do the same. As memories of pain come to mind, take time to process through them with Jesus and with close friends. Ask Jesus to show Himself to you. Ask him where He was when you were facing your tormentors. He has an answer. Of course, I know many readers will need to do this kind of counseling with a trusted friend or professional counselor, and I'd strongly encourage you to do so as needed. However, in your day to day thought life, you may find this practice of asking Jesus where He was in your pain as a first step in your healing journey.

Chapter 11
The Hope of the Righteous

"For God is with the generation of the righteous."
-King David

"Peace on earth, goodwill to men," angelic voices proclaimed above the grazing grounds outside of the quaint town called Bethlehem (Luke 2:14). Their proclamation was heard by only a few and understood by less. This supernatural moment marked the beginning of the well-known Christmas story. Warm feelings of hope and redemption are often speckled with comic relief each time we experience the holiday traditions of nativity scene plays, Christmas carols and gift exchanges. These picturesque moments imprinted into our memories are a joy for us to experience. Our experiences, however, are far from the reality into which the angels announced Jesus' arrival. Did peace truly come to earth? By all historical accounts, no.

The Jews remained under the oppression of Rome the morning following Jesus' miraculous birth. It was a long two years before the wisemen arrived bearing their gifts for the baby Jesus. Upon discovering their reason for visiting his kingdom, King Herod slaughtered all children under the age of two in the Bethlehem province. There was no peace on earth.

When Jesus began His ministry around the age of thirty, Rome's power was in full force. The era of Pax Romana, or "Roman Peace," permeated the ancient world. However, peace for Rome was not synonymous with peace for the Jews. Various rebellions against Rome were instigated, but none prevailed. There was no peace on earth. So, what peace did the angels promise to the shepherds?

This question concerns us as much today as it did the communities of ancient Israel. If the peace wasn't delivered by liberation from Rome, then how did it enter our world? The peace that the angels spoke of was not a political peace, rather it was an offer extended to a restless humanity. It came in the person of Jesus. He invited all who dared to believe Him into a life of eternal peace and purpose.

The cause for all humanity's restlessness and suffering is found in our desire to be like the God who created us. We are children who long to know the comforting, guiding hands of a father. In our broken, opposing nature we are unable to know Him or be like Him. In fact, we are so far from Him that we can hardly recognize His life when we see it. When Jesus came to mankind, as John poetically poses, we "did not know Him. He came to His own, and His own did not receive Him (John 1:10-11).

So, Jesus went the distance and laid dormant His Divine nature to show us how to approach God in our humanity. He showed us how to be the sons and daughters of God. We need only to believe and allow Him to awaken in us His Divine nature.

This is the peace and hope the angels promised. This finish line of

Christian faith is pronounced again by Paul when he writes, "For we through the Spirit eagerly wait for the hope of righteousness by faith" (Galatians 5:5).[46] This hope is a "joyful and confident expectation of eternal salvation." Every believer has an implanted ability to behave out of their righteous identity because Jesus has made this new identity accessible to all who will believe (John 1:12). This Divine ability replaces our need for a condemning moral law. To say it simply, God is counting on the Divine identity He placed in us to pull us out of our human nature. When we see ourselves easily duplicating the loving nature of God, we are fulfilling the "hope of righteousness."

As you can imagine this happening on a personal level, consider what it would be like if entire communities were led by God's righteous identity? I'm not implying the fulfillment of this hope only in an afterlife. Instead, I believe God's intent is for His kingdom to come in this life. As we turn to the scriptures, we can catch glimpses of God's plan.

Throughout the Old Testament, we see many men and women who hoped for a culture defined by God's righteousness. They knew the day would come in which God would fuse His identity into millions of people and this reality would utterly transform the world. The fulfillment of this hope would bring peace on earth. As the identity of God residing in mankind would shape each persons' thought and behavior, a new way of living would emerge.

The author of Hebrews tells us that Abraham "waited for the city which has foundations, whose builder and maker is God" (Hebrews 11:10). The prophets of old saw a time when the nation of Israel and by virtue all those who have the faith of Abraham, would fulfill this hope of righteousness. The prophet Isaiah paints a clear image of how

46 Strong, J. (1995). Enhanced Strong's Lexicon. Woodside Bible Fellowship.

this reality of a righteous community would transpire. He writes,

> The Spirit of the Lord God is upon Me,
> Because the Lord has anointed Me
> To preach good tidings to the poor;
> He has sent Me to heal the brokenhearted,
> To proclaim liberty to the captives,
> And the opening of the prison to those who are bound;
> To proclaim the acceptable year of the Lord,
> And the day of vengeance of our God (Isaiah 61:1-2)

Isaiah begins with decrees of personal healing, liberty and deliverance. These promises, as he continues, are only the beginning of God's plan to restore all things. This proclamation is also taken up by Jesus as His own mission when He began His ministry. Isaiah foretells how the righteous will "rebuild the old ruins," "raise up the former desolations," and "repair the ruined cities," which are the "desolation of many generations."

The non-believers will call this people of righteousness the "servants of our God." They will have "everlasting joy," and their "descendants shall be known." Isaiah continues to describe how, "All who see them shall acknowledge them, that they are the posterity whom the Lord has blessed." He concludes in proclaiming how this will happen. He says, "As the garden causes the things that are sown in it to spring forth, so the Lord God will cause righteousness and praise to spring forth before all the nations" (Isaiah 61:1–11).

This end-time fulfillment is not one which will occur in hidden pockets or dark corners of the world. No, it will happen "before all nations." As God sought to make Israel a people who would model societal relationship with Him, likewise, God is seeking for entire communities who will wholly model His righteous identity to an unrighteous world.

Many hold this hope but place its fulfillment in the afterlife. However, Isaiah, reveals the fulfillment of his prophecy as an occurrence witnessed by unbelievers. This hope of a righteous generation is repeated in places throughout the scriptures. (See Isaiah 49:8-12, Isaiah 58:12-14, Ezekiel 10:36-10-15, Ezekiel 36:34-38, Acts 3:21, Ephesians 1:9-10, Colossians 1:15-20, 2 Corinthians 5:19)

Of course, with regard to end time beliefs, the hope of a worldwide transformation before Jesus' return presents a conflict of beliefs. Some predict the world will only grow darker, spiraling into moral depravity. Where did this sort of dismal foresight originate? It began in the with the rise of dispensational theology in the 1830's through the teachings of John Darby. Darby, to support the idea of a pre-tribulation rapture, departed from centuries of church teachings to formulate a new thesis. He proposed the world, in the last dispensation of grace, would spiral into wickedness and the church will be rescued before the ultimate judgement of God fell upon it.

Without diving too deeply into the arguments for and against dispensationalism, I can summarize Darby's approach in this way; with broad strokes of speculation and selective scriptural support, Darby painted an image of the righteous being overcome by the wicked and Christ returning to rescue His afflicted Church. The scriptures, in contrast, tell of Christ's kingdom which cannot be shaken and a Church who is glorious and powerful in her ability to reform culture.

Dr. William Bell Jr., in his book, A Critical Evaluation of the

Pretribulation Rapture Doctrine in Christian Eschatology, opposed Darby in saying he, "…arrive(d) at premature literal interpretations of Old Testament passages with insufficient attention being given to the applicable New Testament passages."[47] Translation? Darby's theory took Old Testament scriptures out of context and discarded New Testament passages.

Before dispensationalism spread through theological circles, Church doctrines spoke to the idea of a series of Covenants between God and men. Men like Adam, Noah, Abraham, Moses and David were recipients of God's covenant. Following this, God made a covenant with the church. His covenant with the Church was His unfailing companionship with us as we make disciples.

If we hold to covenant theology, we can clearly see our role in the end. We have work to do and as we succeed in bringing the hope of righteousness to the world, the end will draw near. To believe the world will decline into utter wickedness deflates any hope of cultural transformation. In my opinion, if we hold to a belief that mankind will only get worse, we hopelessly attribute greater power to the forces of evil than to the power of the gospel.

End Time Predictions

Today, each time a world-wide scare occurs, I cannot help but note the patterns of fear and overreaction. Whether it is the tremors of war in the Middle East, natural disasters, or threatening pandemics, it seems the end time prophets are stirred to chant louder their dismal song of, "The end is near." While this an understandable reaction, it seems the doomsday perspective of many leaders has resulted in a neutralizing effect on the church.

---

47 William Everett Bell, Jr., "A Critical Evaluation of the Pretribulation Rapture Doctrine in Christian Eschatology" (Ph.D. diss., New York University, School of Education, 1967), ii-iii.

The fear of a coming destruction seem to draw the Church away from its primary purpose. What should our driving purpose be? We are brought into God's kingdom to reconcile the world, the entire world, back to Jesus (2 Corinthians 5:19).

Two Stories in One

Looking at the scriptures we find that there are two narratives happening during the last days. One is a story of a world rebelling against its Creator. In this plot God allows the consequences of wickedness to catch up with the wicked. But in contrast, the other side of this story tells of Christ's Church rising in power to bring the masses into a relationship with Him. These two prophetic forecasts, while seemingly opposite each other, appear to be concurrent. This dual natured prophetic fulfillment happens often in scriptures. It is best seen in the first advent of Jesus.

First century Jewish rabbis had conflicting predictions as to the location from which the Messiah would emerge. From Isaiah's scroll, they read He would come from Capernaum, also known as the land of Zebulun and Naphtali (Isaiah 9:1-2, Matthew 4:15). The disciple Matthew indicated the Messiah was expected to come out of Egypt as he referenced the prophet Hosea. (Matthew 2:15, Hosea 11:1). Finally, the prophet Micah predicted how Messiah would rise out of Bethlehem (Micah 5:2).

Each prediction was fulfilled, but only in retrospect can we see their validity. Jesus was born in Bethlehem, but shortly after was taken to Egypt. From there He returned to Nazareth around the age of four. Following His launch into the ministry, He made his home in Capernaum (Matthew 4:13). It's interesting to see how one would need to closely examine the life of Jesus, as the disciples did, to realize how these apparent contradicting prophesies were fulfilled. As we look to Christ's second advent, it is no surprise to see a similar pattern.

The contradicting prophecies, as I noted before, are of a world falling into a state of deplorable morality and of a church rising in great power to redeem the world. How can both happen? It can only happen as God reveals His righteous nature through the lives of those who follow Him.

Hope in the Midst of Hell

As we hear predictions of the end times with a bias toward a moral implosion, the hope of redemption is often lost. In a practical sense, if the followers of Jesus feel powerless to transform communities, their focus will be drawn away from the work God desires to do. We cannot lose the hope we have been given of a world that will see and experience Jesus because of a vibrant Church.

In looking at Christ's end time prediction in Matthew 24:1-31, He urges us to work toward the benchmark of global discipleship. Crossing this finish line of world-wide discipleship, we find it to be the precursor to the world's end. Let's dive deeper into this passage of Jesus' prediction. Before He gives this prophecy, He was led on a grand tour of the temple mount by his disciples. They were peacock proud of their holy site, and as expected, Jesus popped their inflated zeal by saying, "Do you not see all these things? Assuredly, I say to you, not one stone shall be left here upon another, that shall not be thrown down" (Matthew 24:1).

I'm sure they were hurt and maybe even a little offended by Jesus' words. They asked Him three questions to gain some footing in response to His prediction. They asked, "Tell us, when will these things be? And what will be the sign of Your coming, and of the end of the age?"

Jesus responded by defining the condition of the world, which will indicate the "beginning of sorrows." What were these indicators? War, famine, pestilence (diseases), and earthquakes will come. Jesus says when we see these things, "the end is not yet," but these disasters are only "beginning of sorrows" (Matthew 24:6-7).

Jesus continues by saying tribulation will come to his followers. Now before you're triggered by the word tribulation, note what He says in Matthew 24:9-10: "Then they will deliver you up to tribulation and kill you, and all nations will hate you for My name's sake. And then many will be offended, will betray one another, and will hate one another." This prediction has been occurring since the birth of the church. The Christian faith was born in persecution. It grows in the face of persecution, and by all historical measures, it also becomes the most potent and beautiful under the trying hand of persecution. To believe Christian faith flourishes best in peace and tranquility betrays an ignorance of Church history.

When we hear the word *tribulation*, many imagine a fearful scenario of believers running, desperately trying to preserve their lives . But this is not the correct imagery for this word. The Greek term for tribulation is "thlisipn." It is better translated as "distress." There will be distress among Jesus' disciples, but we shouldn't forget the promises God gave us in times of distress. The scriptures encourage us by saying,

We are hard-pressed on every side, yet not crushed; we are

perplexed, but not in despair; persecuted, but not forsaken; struck down, but not destroyed - always carrying about in the body the dying of the Lord Jesus, that the life of Jesus also may be manifested in our body. For we who live are always delivered to death for Jesus' sake, that the life of Jesus also may be manifested in our mortal flesh. (2 Corinthians 4:8–11)

An accurate word picture for the term tribulation is that of grapes being pressed to produce wine. Is it possible that the distressing tribulation which many dread is actually the process by which the church will develop into the beautiful bride Jesus desires? This tribulation, I believe, may not be a punishment as much as refining work. Again, looking at church history, believers have endured tribulations for centuries.

Concluding His prediction of this coming time, Jesus gave us the other side of the story. He says, "This gospel of the kingdom will be preached in all the world as a witness to all the nations, and then the end will come" (Matthew 24:14). The hope we have is one of global discipleship. The end of the story is how the church will take the good news of God's kingdom throughout the world. Every ethnic group across the face of the earth will hear about the righteous identity they can possess. Following this, the end will begin.

In responding to the question of when Jerusalem would be destroyed, Jesus foretold of the rise of the "abomination of desolation." This leader is defined by many as the Antichrist. With his ascent to power, Jesus told how there would be "great tribulation" (Matt 24:21). However, this period will be brief; Jesus implied it would possibly only be a few years. Fulfilling this prophecy, in 66 AD, the Jews rebelled against Roman occupation. The Emperor Nero responded by sending out armies under the leadership of Vespasian to squelch the rebellion. "By 68 AD, Jewish resistance in the northern part of Israel had been eradicated and the Romans turned their full attention to the subjugation of Jerusalem. That same year, the Emperor Nero died by his own hand, creating a power vacuum in Rome.

In the resulting chaos, Vespasian was declared Emperor and returned to the Imperial City. It fell to his son, Titus, to lead the remaining army in the assault on Jerusalem. Roman legions surrounded the city and began to slowly squeeze the life out of the Jewish stronghold. By 70 A.D. the Romans breached Jerusalem's outer walls and began a systematic ransacking of the city. The assault culminated in the burning and destruction of the Temple..."[48]

Leaders within the church remembered Jesus' warning and immediately fled into the mountains when the assault began. "Pious Jews considered the Christian flight to be an act of treason. This sealed the fate of the of the Church in the Jewish world."[49] Eusebius, an early church historian, tells us the Christians fled to Pella in Perea when the Roman army appeared and began to surround Jerusalem."[50] The hope Jesus gave in the midst of this time of tribulation was a promise of the gospel reaching every ethnic group in the world. As predicted, the fleeing Christians spread throughout the known Middle Eastern World. Since that time to this, the church's commission has been to take the message of God's kingdom around world.

Jesus' use of the phrase "abomination of desolation," links us to a parallel prophecy and fulfillment. The title of "abomination of desolation," violently marked the history of every Jewish listener in Jesus' day. The title was initially used by the Old Testament prophet Daniel

48 http://www.eyewitnesstohistory.com/jewishtemple.htm
49 Shelley, Bruce L. (1982,1995) Church History in Plain English (2nd Edition, p. 23)
50 Utley, R. J. (2000). The First Christian Primer: Matthew (Vol. Volume 9, p. 199). Marshall, TX: Bible Lessons International.

(Daniel 11:31). After Daniel gave his prophecy, it was fulfilled by Antiochus Epiphanies IV in 168 BC. Antiochus erected an altar to the Greek god Zeus in the temple and sacrificed a pig on it. This was a direct affront to the people of God. However, just as there was a parallel redemption to Jesus' prediction, Daniel prophesied how, "the people who know their God shall be strong and carry out great exploits."

In the fulfillment of Daniel's words, when Antiochus Epiphanies IV defiled the temple, Judas Maccabeus rose up to lead the Judeans to miraculous victories. The greatest of them was a battle of 6,000 Jews against Antiochus and his 40,000 soldiers. Judas and his men fasted, prayed and repented before the battle. As a result of God's favor, the Jews prevailed.

Following their triumph, Judas entered Jerusalem and re-consecrated the Temple. He cleansed it and a new altar was built. New holy vessels were fashioned. When they searched for oil to light the menorah, they found that most of it had been contaminated by the Syrians. There was only one container which remained sealed. There was only enough oil in it to burn the menorah for a day, but the oil miraculously lasted for eight days. During that length of time, they were able to prepare a lasting supply of oil. As a result, the eight-day festival of Hanukkah was instituted to commemorate this miracle. Following this victory, faithful Jews were free to worship and practice their faith. [51]

In both predictions of a rising antichrist, we maintain the hope of the righteous rising in the face of persecution. Daniel's prophesy foretold how "the people who do know their God shall be strong and do exploits." (Daniel 11:32). Jesus predicted how the "gospel of the

51 https://www.biblewise.com/bible_study/characters/judas-maccabeus.php

kingdom shall be preached in the whole world as a testimony to all the nations" (Matthew 24:14).

As a disciple of Jesus today, how should we respond to these end time passages? Should we campaign to promote our end-time view in church circles? Should we stockpile food and ammunition to prepare for the rise of the antichrist? Should we run up credit cards and live luxuriously, hoping for a painless transition into glory. Don't laugh, there are many believers who have endorsed such sentiments. If we look at Jesus' words, we can find helpful directives.

Jesus followed His prophecy with this-is-what-you-do parables. His parable of the fig tree tells us to pay attention to what is happening in the world (Matthew 24:32-35). Jesus also references the story of Noah's flood. As it came to pass in Noah's day, He indicates how we will not know exactly when the end is coming. In His parable of the men and women busily at work and story of the foolish servant, He tells us His return will be a surprise to all (Matthew 24:40-44).

In His parable of the wise and foolish virgins and of a master returning to his entrusted servants, His theme of a surprise return and a subsequent evaluation continues (Matthew 24:45- 25:30). In each story we see the reward of those whose righteous identity led them to be vigilant and wise. Those who lacked this new identity were condemned because they grew complacent and did not value what they possessed.

Jesus' message was clear: We all will give an account for the life we have lived. If you take your salvation for granted, there will be consequences. This godly lifestyle we have been given is designed to transform the world. If we minimize our salvation to mere moral decision, there is cost for our neglect. As you and I live out our righteous identity we can, and will, see entire communities transformed by the freedom Jesus offers.

We must finish the work He began. Every people group must see men and women of God living in the fullness of their righteous identity. This is the great promise the world is waiting to experience, and it is the reason for the hope we possess (Romans 8:19). In his book entitled Ethics, Dietrich Bonhoeffer speaks to this promise of humanity's transformation in saying,

> In the body of Jesus Christ, God is united with humankind, all humanity is accepted by God, and the world is reconciled to God. In the body of Jesus Christ, God took on the sin of all the world and bore it. There is no part of the world, no matter how lost, no matter how godless, that has not been accepted by God in Jesus Christ and reconciled to God.[52]

The Psalmist David looking through the ages gives us a glimpse of this reformation when he writes,

> Who may ascend into the hill of the Lord?
> Or who may stand in His holy place?
> He who has clean hands and a pure heart,
> Who has not lifted up his soul to an idol,
> Nor sworn deceitfully.
> He shall receive blessing from the Lord,
> And righteousness from the God of his salvation.
> This is Jacob, the generation of those who seek Him,
> Who seek Your face. (Psalms 24:3-6)

---

52 Dietrich Bonhoeffer, Ethics (New York: Touchstone, 1995), p.66–68.

The author of Hebrews also shows us how the righteous identity of God transformed the nation of Israel as it was conferred upon a handful of individuals. He says,

> And what more shall I say? For the time would fail me to tell of Gideon and Barak and Samson and Jephthah, also of David and Samuel and the prophets: who through faith subdued kingdoms, worked righteousness, obtained promises, stopped the mouths of lions, quenched the violence of fire, escaped the edge of the sword, out of weakness were made strong, became valiant in battle, turned to flight the armies of the aliens. Women received their dead raised to life again. (Hebrews 11:32-34)

If reformations were brought about through the lives of these few individuals, though they lived with a partial understanding of God's righteousness, how much more can an entire Church do with the indwelling Sprit of God? As the author continues, he says,

> And all these, having obtained a good testimony through faith, did not receive the promise, God having provided something better for us, that they should not be made perfect apart from us. Therefore we also, since we are surrounded by so great a cloud of witnesses, let us lay aside every weight, and the sin which so easily ensnares us, and let us run with endurance the race that is set before us, looking unto Jesus, the author and finisher of our faith, who for the joy that was set before Him endured the cross, despising the shame, and has sat down at the right hand of the throne of God. (Hebrews 11:39–12:2)

We are given a much better covenant than the Old testament patriarchs. They looked forward to the day when their hope for God's reign in the earth would be reality. Their hope is left for us to accomplish. Their hope was for a time when God's identity would be found in entire cultures throughout the world.

Peace on Earth

Through the years of counseling families within the church, at times I have been overwhelmed with grief. My hope in the ability of God's righteous identity to change a darkened heart is often discouraged. I've gone into a session with hope like a raging fire. I've began with a confidence in God's ability to liberate the drug addict, the porn bound teen, the anger-controlled dad or abusive mom. Then as I hear their life-wrecking stories my hope is often deflated.

I've exited my office many times with all my hope extinguished by despair. It is especially in those moments that I bow my head, wipe away the tears of sorrow, and look forward to the day when the righteous identity of Jesus will be evident in entire communities throughout the world.

A few years ago, I sat with a young man who told me of the horrendous abuse his wife had endured at the hands of her father. The shame, deception and perversion shook me deeply. As this husband's story concluded, my eyes filled with tears. All I could think was, "God, how could such evil happen? Could this wife be healed? Could this man's marriage be restored? Could this girl's father be saved?"

As I left my office late that winter evening, I sorrowfully climbed in my truck and turned on the ignition. On the radio played a Christmas song declaring peace on earth. The song, I later learned, began as a poem by Henry Wadsworth Longfellow. Longfellow penned it in 1863. A few years prior, he traumatically lost his wife in a house fire. Not only did the flames rob him of his bride, but it disfigured his face in his rescue attempt. Then his son, after enlisting in the first Massachusetts artillery against Longfellow's will, was wounded. Henry made the arduous journey to retrieve his battle-wounded son.

As the Christmas season was upon him, the burden of his losses took a toll on his soul. On December 8, 1963, as he sat broken by his family tragedies and weighed under the oppression of a nation at war. In that moment he heard the bells of Christmas ring. Their resonance inspired an eternal hope as Henry wrote,

> And in despair I bowed my head;
> "There is no peace on earth," I said:
> "For hate is strong,
> And mocks the song
> Of peace on earth, good-will to men!"
> Then pealed the bells more loud and deep:
> "God is not dead; nor does He sleep!
> The Wrong shall fail
> The Right prevail,
> With peace on earth, good-will to men!"

As I listened to those words sung triumphantly on that cold, winter evening, I found comfort in the promise they made. The right will prevail. The wrong will fail. My despairing soul found the same hope in which Longfellow rested. God's ever-present nature will set aright the evils we endure. How will He do this? It will be through those who carry His redeeming identity in this broken world.

We have a reason for hope because it is God's nature we are given. This promise is not a naïve, wishful expectation. We can hold to the hope of an entire generation being made righteous because of the power of God's identity can be in us. This is the inevitable end of God's work through the lives of those who love Him.

Appendix

Theories on the Dating of Galatians

Theory One

If the Galatia region addressed by Paul lay in southern Turkey, then Paul's first missionary journey to these southern cities are reflected in Acts 13–14 making this his first letter to the church.[53] This letter would have preceded Paul's appearance before the Jerusalem council in Acts 15, or it may have been written shortly after meeting with the apostles. This theory would yield itself to another reason why Paul may have sensed the need to defend his authority as an apostle. (Gal. 1:1) Following his first journey, Paul was validated as an apostle by the mother church in Jerusalem and such explanation possibly would not have been necessary. This first theory places Paul's writing of this epistle around 49 A.D.

Theory Two

If Paul wrote to the Galatians in the Northern part of Turkey, his letter would be dated in the middle to late fifties during his second or third missionary journey. Paul's traveling companions would be Silas and Timothy.[54] In the context of this geography, some have linked Paul's illness in Galatians 4:13 to malaria. There is an assumption that Paul may have traveled north into the highlands to escape the marshy, malaria-infested, coastal lowlands.[55]

Theory Three

The Third: If Paul wrote his letter before his visit to the Jerusalem Council, then "Galatians 2:1–10 describes Paul and Barnabas' visit to Jerusalem as described in Acts 11:30 and 12:25. This theory also

53 Utley, R. J. (1997). Paul's First Letters: Galatians and I & II Thessalonians (Vol. Volume 11, pp. 1–2). Marshall, TX: Bible Lessons International.
54 Ibid
55 Ibid

supports the belief of this epistle being the earliest of his epistles. According to this theory, the revelation mentioned (Gal 2:2) corresponds with the prophecy of Agabus (Acts 11:27–28). This view holds that the private speaking about the gospel shared among the Gentiles precludes the Acts 15 visit but fits perfectly with Acts 11. It further holds that continuing to remember the poor (Gal. 2: 10) fits with the purpose of the Acts 11 visit, but not Acts 15." If this theory holds true, then Galatians could have been written even earlier than the 49 A.D.

About the Author

Pastor Samuel serves as the executive pastor at Community Church in Orange, TX. He has a passion for preaching the gospel and his teachings compel audiences to leave behind a nominal faith and pursue a life of encountering Jesus. With years of travel into unreached nations, Stephen's global perspective provides a unique approach to unfolding the Scriptures and communicating Biblical truths. Along with his wife, Jenilee, and their four boys, they have witnessed God's direction as they've cultivated effective avenues of ministry.

Stephen completed his BBA in economics at Lamar University and his doctorate in theology from the Midwest College of Theology. He is also ordained with the Assemblies of God and has served with various mission organizations. Stephen and Jenilee are directors of Free Life Missions, a non-profit mission organization.

Made in the USA
Coppell, TX
10 December 2020